# Juan Ponce de León

# JUAN PONCE DE LEON

*by Nina Brown Baker*

ILLUSTRATED BY ROBERT DOREMUS

jB
P773b

New York *Alfred A Knopf* 1957

*L. C. catalog card number: 57-7082*

© NINA BROWN BAKER, 1957

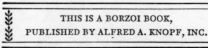

THIS IS A BORZOI BOOK,
PUBLISHED BY ALFRED A. KNOPF, INC.

FIRST EDITION

*For Margaret Lee*

# Contents

# Juan Ponce de León

# The Boy at the Gate

DON Pedro Nuñez de Guzman, Lord of Teruel, finished his dinner and leaned back with a sigh of content. It had been a good dinner, especially welcome after a hard day of hunting. Now, full-fed and pleasantly weary, he was ready for bed.

He was about to rise when he remembered the letter. He had thrust it carelessly into his belt, and forgotten it. In the early morning that had been, just as he rode out through the castle gate.

A boy had waylaid him there; a shabby lad standing beside a bony, starved-looking horse. The boy had held out the letter and tried to say something. Don Pedro took the paper with a careless "Later, later!" Waving the youth aside, he rode on.

Now he unfolded the letter, spreading it out under the nearest candle. A look of surprise crossed his face as he saw the signature. Father Santiago, his old teacher! It had been years since he had heard of him. Now, it appeared, he was parish priest of a distant village. What could he want of his old pupil?

Don Pedro hurried through the letter. Then he turned to the page behind his chair.

"There was a boy at the gate this morning," he said. "Do you know anything of him?"

The page bowed. "Yes, your grace. He is still there. The guards told him to go away, but he says your grace will want to see him. He seems very sure of himself, my lord. The guards do not think he is a common beggar."

"No, that he is not. Well, I'll see him now. Find him, and bring him to me."

Don Pedro helped himself to a peach from the silver dish. He was halfway through it when the door opened. The young stranger appeared in the opening.

He halted there, bowed, and said: "Juan Ponce de León of San Servos, your grace. Yours to command."

Night had fallen. The shadows were deep around the doorway. The dim light was kind to the threadbare doublet, to the patched and darned trunk hose, the cracked boots. These signs of poverty were cruelly clear as Don Pedro beckoned him into the candle glow.

"I'm sorry you had so long a wait," the knight said kindly. "You should have explained your mission to my men. They would have made you comfortable."

The boy flushed. "My mission is to ask a favor of your grace," he said quietly. "If you refuse me, it is not necessary for others to know I have been rejected. I did not mind the waiting."

"A proper pride, I see." Don Pedro nodded approvingly. "As I might have expected from one of Ponce blood. Well, now, to this mission of yours. You want to enter my service. Father Santiago recommends you. He says you have quick wits, and courage, and ambition. You hope to rise in the world. And your family situation is such that there is no opportunity for you in San Servos."

He lifted his keen eyes to the boy. "Just what is the family situation that holds you back?"

"It is this, my lord. We Ponces of San Servos are a noble family fallen into decay. My ancestor married a princess of León, adding her name to ours. Once we owned castles, and lands, and riches beyond counting. But all that was in ages past. There is nothing left. Nothing!"

"I know," Don Pedro cut in. "It is the same with many a proud family of Aragon. Too many nobles, too few peasants to till the soil. And always, always too many wars to lay our poor land waste! Well, to your immediate family, boy. Your father is dead?"

"And my mother, sir. I have grown up in the care of a great-aunt. There are no male Ponces left. No one to teach me the arts of war. No one to follow as a boy should follow a knight. There *are* no knights at San Servos, my lord! It is a wretched ruined village of old women and goats, with our ancient castle crumbling about our heads. I cannot stay there, and I will not! I begged Father Santiago to help me get away. He sent me to you."

"Why to me?" Don Pedro asked. "If memory serves me, you have a powerful kinsman. Don Rodrigo Ponce de León is one of the King's most trusted generals. He is a distant relation, it is true, but you are of his blood. Surely he would help you?"

"I would rather die than ask his help." The young voice quivered with anger. "Long ago, when I was a baby, my great-aunt appealed to Don Rodrigo. He did not even have the courtesy to reply. While I live, I shall ask nothing of that man!"

"Well, it's true that Don Rodrigo is not noted for kindness of heart," Don Pedro answered. "A brave man, but a cold and selfish one, from what I know of him."

"I want nothing of him," Juan repeated. "Father Santiago says that you are my one best hope. It is hard for a Ponce to plead, my lord. But if you can find it in your heart to take me, I will serve you well."

"Let us think about this. You wish to become a knight?"

"What else?" the boy's chin lifted proudly.

"The Ponces have always been knights. I would win glory on the battlefield, as my fathers have done before me. There is no other life worth living."

Don Pedro frowned. "You are how old? Fifteen? And you have not learned to handle a sword? You have never ridden in a tourney? I fear you have left it too late, my boy. A knight's education should begin at seven, not fifteen."

"Your grace," Juan said steadily, "I told you there was no one to teach me the arts of war. I did not say I was completely ignorant of them. I have a sword—the one my grandfather carried in the French war. And I have a horse, such as the poor creature is. What I could teach myself by long practice I have learned. I know it is very little. But I do not think your grace would find me a stupid pupil."

The knight's stern face softened. He liked the way this shabby boy spoke up for himself. Much though it meant to him, young Juan was too proud to cringe and flatter. Perhaps he was worth helping.

"Well, we shall see," Don Pedro said mildly. "I must think it over. Let us leave your affairs for the moment. I want to hear all about dear old Father

Santiago. Is he well? Is he content in the village you dislike so much? Does he—but wait. You have missed your dinner. Sit down. I'll have a glass of wine with you. We can talk as you eat."

Gratefully the boy sank into the armchair across the table. He had not eaten since noontime, when he finished the last of his bread and cheese. But he ate the rich food daintily, displaying the table manners of a Spanish nobleman. Watching him, Don Pedro's approval grew. This was no country bumpkin. Properly dressed, young Ponce would not disgrace him in any company.

Juan finished his meal and waited in silence. Don Pedro spoke slowly.

"I have not the time or patience to train a beginner, Juan. Your only use to me at present would be as a page. You would help the boys who keep my clothes in order, polish my boots, serve my meals. They are all younger than you. At your age, you should be a squire. That is not possible until you have some military training. My master-at-arms would see to that. When I do not need you, he could give you lessons. Later, if he thinks well of you—but that depends on yourself. You would have to start very low, my boy. You are starting very late. If you rise, you must rise by your own efforts."

"I ask nothing better, my lord," Juan said eagerly. "If I cannot rise by my own efforts, I do not deserve to rise."

The knight's sharp eyes swept his face.

"A page's duties may not please you, Juan. Will that Ponce pride stoop to carrying out my shaving water? To bundling my soiled linen for the laundress? Think well before you choose, my boy."

"Any duties your grace can ask will please me, my lord. Pride—yes, we Ponces have pride. But it is the pride of service. We serve Holy Church, we serve our King, we serve our lord. Whatever service is asked, we are proud to give. It is with pride that I shall serve your grace in the lowliest of duties."

Don Pedro smiled. "You have an eloquent tongue in your head, young fellow. It will not hurt you in this rise of yours. No, it will not hurt. It is settled, then."

He turned to the page who had stood silently at his elbow throughout the long conversation.

"Carlos, you will take Juan with you while you prepare my bed. Show him what is to be done. He will assist as you help me undress. Then you may take him to the pages' quarters and find him a place to sleep."

Twelve-year-old Carlos, splendid in his silk doublet and hose, ventured one disdainful glance at Juan's patches and darns. Then, with a respectful "Yes, my lord," he led the way out of the chamber.

Don Pedro helped himself to another peach and thoughtfully poured another glass of wine. Had he been foolish to burden himself with this untrained youth? It would be hard to refuse a request from good old Father Santiago.

"If I cannot rise by my own efforts, I do not deserve to rise"—he liked the spirit in those words.

"No, I do not think I have been foolish," the Lord of Teruel told himself.

# Off to the Wars

JUAN Ponce de León remained a page for only a few months. The sergeant who was teaching him the soldier's craft was amazed at his progress. The boy was a natural horseman, he reported. And he handled his clumsy old-fashioned sword as though he had been born with it in his hand.

Don Pedro Nuñez himself was known as the finest swordsman in all Aragon. He was interested enough to propose a fencing match between Juan and one of his young officers. The officer won, as was natural. But Juan's performance was so good that the sergeant spoke bluntly to his master.

"You see how it is, your grace. It's a shame to waste a lad like that on household tasks. Give him to me, and I'll make a soldier of him in six months. He has a lot to learn. I can't teach him much in the few hours he has free. But he's the fastest learner I've ever seen. He devours his lessons as though they were cake! He's a born soldier, your lordship. I can make you proud of him."

"Do you mean you'd take him into the guard?" Don Pedro asked doubtfully. "He's of noble blood you know, Sergeant. Would he agree to serve as a common soldier?"

"He would, and gladly," the sergeant answered. "I've talked to the lad. He wants it that way. He says no officer is fit to command men until he's been through the ranks himself. That's not the way most of these young aristocrats talk, and your honor knows what poor officers we get. Young Master Ponce won't stay long in the ranks, sir. You give him to me now, and I'll give you back a captain before the New Year."

"You really think so well of him?" Don Pedro

asked. "I've had the same feeling—this is no ordinary boy. Well, have it your way, Sergeant. Teach him all you can, and turn him back to me. I think he's worth keeping under my own eye for the next few years."

As a full-time soldier, Juan did even better than the sergeant had predicted. He did so well that in a few months Don Pedro chose him for his own squire.

This was a high honor. The castle was full of young officers, but the lord's personal squire was someone very special.

It meant that Juan was constantly at Don Pedro's side, on foot or horseback. He sat with him at table, mingling with his guests as an equal. He would ride with his master in battle. If he did well in the field, he could hope to be made a knight. It was a bright prospect for the boy who had come to the castle practically as a beggar.

No one would have recognized that beggar now. Juan wore with equal grace the silks and velvets of the castle, and the shining armor of the tournament. He was tall and broad-shouldered, with a high-bridged aristocratic nose which some thought he carried too high in the air. Don Pedro did not think so. He was a proud man himself, and he admired pride in others. The good knight saw in the father-less boy the son he had never had. He gave Juan a father's affection, and it was gratefully returned.

His first years with Don Pedro were years of peace. The young squire went with his patron to Valladolid for the wedding of Ferdinand of Aragon and Isabella of Castile. Nineteen years old then, he danced with the bridesmaids and took part in the military review which was part of the festivities. And not long afterward, he followed Don Pedro into battle.

The marriage of the two sovereigns united Aragon and Castile into the kingdom we know as Spain. Their first years together were years of turmoil. Affonso V, King of Portugal, claimed he had a better right to the throne of Castile than Isabella. He fought a war to prove it. Don Pedro Nuñez de Guzman plunged into the thick of the fighting, his squire at his side. We do not know just what Juan Ponce de León did to distinguish himself at the battle of Toro. But it must have been something unusually brave, for he received his knight-hood there at King Ferdinand's hands.

Juan's place in Don Pedro's service changed

now. He was a knight himself, with a squire of his own. But the kind nobleman who was his second father could not bear to lose him. Juan became a captain in Don Pedro's private army.

The army system of that day was very different from ours. Every great lord had an army of his own, raised from among the peasants on his estate. When the King called upon him, he brought his army to the service of the nation. But the lord himself was supreme commander of his own forces. His men were responsible to him alone.

Don Pedro had a very good army. With Juan on the staff, it became even better. The young knight's experience in the ranks gave him a rare knowledge of how the ordinary soldier felt. In peace or in war, the men trusted him and followed willingly where he led.

The Portuguese war was won, but a greater war was soon to follow. King Ferdinand scarcely gave the country a breathing spell before the drums sounded again. This time, the King meant to drive the Moors from their last foothold in Spain.

It had been centuries now since the Moors first crossed over from Africa to conquer Spain. Once they had held the entire peninsula. Over the years

they had been pushed back, until now they pos-
sessed only the southern province of Granada.
There they remained, defying any attempt to dis-
lodge them. Ferdinand thought the time had come
for a final effort.

The Portuguese war had not been too popular.
Many of the Spanish nobles had sided with Affonso,
and refused to fight for Isabella's rights. But the war
to liberate Granada was a different matter. This was
a struggle of Christian against Moslem, a religious
crusade in which Spanish success became the triumph of the Cross.

All Christians, in those days before the Protestant
Reformation, were Catholics. Isabella and Ferdinand were so devout that the Pope gave them the
title of "the Catholic Sovereigns." He blessed the
Moorish war, sending a silver cross to carry beside
the royal standard.

The nobles of Aragon and Castile, whatever
their private quarrels, united to follow the cross
into Granada. Christian knights from England,
France, and Germany flocked to join the holy war.
Before it ended, the Catholic Sovereigns could
count on a force of 80,000 men.

They needed them all. The Moors were entrenched in rock-built fortresses against which horsemen threw themselves in vain. But Ferdinand was a resourceful soldier, as well as a brave one. He set his engineers to building clumsy cannon which fired heavy stone balls against the stone walls. And one by one the Moorish fortresses crumbled before the Christian tide.

It was a long, slow business. Ten bloody years passed between the first battle and the final surrender. The two rulers scarcely left the front in all that time. King Ferdinand personally led every important assault. His wife was never far from his side.

Queen Isabella planned her own duties. She saw to it that provisions reached the troops, and that the men were made as comfortable as possible. She arranged to have the wounded cared for, and Masses said for the dead. It is no wonder that she had small time to spare for an Italian adventurer named Christopher Columbus, who wanted her to send him off to find India.

The Moorish king, Boabdil, had a gorgeous palace in Granada called the Alhambra. He surrendered it to Ferdinand and Isabella on January 2, 1492. As a Spanish poet put it: "Here passed away the Koran; there in the Cross was borne; And here was heard the Christian bell; and dumb the Moorish horn."

In the round of celebrations that followed the victory, the Queen found time to think of Columbus. He was summoned to Granada. There at last he received the royal permission to search for a western route to India. The promise was solemnly made before all the assembled court. It is not known whether or not Juan Ponce de León was present for that historic scene.

He may well have been. His patron, Don Pedro, had just been appointed military tutor to Their Majesties' young son. This was a reward for Don Pedro's gallant accomplishments in the war. Juan had served under his command. Later, when Ponce became famous, his biographers would say that "he displayed daring and enterprise against the Moors." Unfortunately, no details are given.

There is another Ponce de León who was a hero of the Moorish war. Juan's haughty kinsman, General Rodrigo Ponce de León, did so well that the King made him Marquis of Cadiz. He is known to have been present at the audience granted to Columbus. Legend says that he advised against the expedition.

Don Rodrigo's advice was not heeded. Columbus sailed away to find the New World. The Marquis of Cadiz died in that same year. He and the military glory he won are long forgotten. He would never know that the name of Ponce de León would live, not for him, but for the cousin he had ignored. He could not have dreamed that that name would become immortal in the New World which Columbus was to add to the map.

No one could have dreamed it then. And the last person to foresee it would surely have been Captain Juan, who had never left his native Spain, and never expected to.

# Beyond the Western Sea

DON Pedro was waiting for him in the garden of the royal palace at Barcelona. Juan had not seen his patron since the Moorish surrender. Don Pedro had followed the court to Barcelona. Juan had remained in Granada with the army of occupation.

The meeting between them now was a warm one.

"Sit down, my boy," Don Pedro said after the first greetings. He gestured toward the marble bench from which he had risen. It was a pleasant spot, shaded by an orange tree heavy with fruit.

"I have the afternoon free," he went on. "Her Majesty has taken my pupil to Assumption Convent to visit his great-aunt, who is Mother Superior there."

"And how is the young prince?" Juan asked politely. "Are you making a soldier of him, sir?"

"I do my best." The old man sighed. "He is a frail child, Juan, and exercise tires him cruelly. It will break his father's heart if—but there, I must not gossip about my master's family affairs. Tell me of yourself. How do you find life in Granada?"

"I find it dull," Juan answered bluntly. "You will remember that after the beaten Moorish armies withdrew to Africa, Their Majesties gave the civilians a choice. They could follow, or they could remain. But if they chose to stay, they must give up their Moslem religion and become Christians. Some families made one choice, some the other."

"So I have heard. It all goes on very peacefully, they tell me."

"Peacefully indeed," Juan answered. "The quartermasters have been busy evacuating those who wanted to go. The priests have had their hands full instructing and baptizing the converts. Neither lot has put up any sort of fight. There's nothing for the military to do but to look on."

Don Pedro smiled. "No life for an ambitious soldier, is it? I thought you would be feeling that. It's why I sent for you. I have something new in mind for you, Juan."

"Have you, my lord?" The young man's eyes sparkled. "You can't know how glad I am to hear those words. No news comes to us at Granada. Is there to be a new war somewhere?"

"No, not a war, exactly." Don Pedro hesitated. "You say news did not come to you at Granada. But you must have heard of Admiral Columbus and his discoveries in the Indies? All Spain has been buzzing with excitement since his return."

"I've heard something," Juan answered. "But it's such an amazing story I find it hard to believe. Like everyone else, I thought we'd seen the last of the Admiral when he sailed out into the Western Ocean. Then, this spring, we heard he had returned in triumph. They say he brought a cargo of savages and strange colored birds, and gold and pearls. Are you telling me that it is all true?"

"It is indeed," Don Pedro replied. "I have seen his Indian captives with my own eyes. And the birds called parrots, which have been taught to speak Spanish, so you would think they had human tongues. Many other strange and wonderful treasures he brought, too. Golden trinkets and a net full of pearls. Fruits such as never grew in civilized lands. But all these things you will see for yourself. It is not of them I wish to speak."

He paused a minute, gathering his thoughts. Juan hid his impatience and waited respectfully.

"The Admiral claimed the new-found land for Spain," Don Pedro went on at last. "He now proposes to set up a Spanish colony there. He is gathering a grand fleet of seventeen ships. They will carry carpenters and stone masons with their tools. Her Majesty is providing furnishings for a church, which is to be the first permanent building. Among the company will be many skilled miners. The Admiral reports that the natives know nothing of mining. Although there is gold beneath their soil, they value it only as ornament, and are equally happy with a string of sea shells. They will labor willingly, but there must be Spanish miners to direct their efforts."

"No doubt," Juan agreed. He looked a little puzzled. This was all very interesting, but what had it to do with him? He was neither a builder nor a miner.

Don Pedro saw his bewilderment, and laughed. "You are wondering when I shall come to my point? Well, here it is. The Admiral reports that the natives are a timid, docile lot who will give us no trouble. This may be so, or it may not be. Our lord the King has his doubts. His Majesty is a soldier, as the Admiral is not. He thinks it wise to send a military company to enforce Spanish authority in the islands. Now do you see? How would you like to command a troop in New Spain?"

"Can you ask that? It would be the most exciting adventure of my life!" Juan said eagerly. "But—surely every officer in Spain must be clamoring for the honor. Could it really come to me?"

"It will not come easily," Don Pedro warned. "As you have guessed, His Majesty is being besieged with requests. You see it as adventure. But to most men, the lure is that of treasure. Gold and pearls to be had for the taking—oh, that is a prospect to excite the greed in many hearts! They give our gracious King no rest, these eager volunteers. The officers he chooses will leave some bitter enemies behind them."

"If I am chosen, I shall not worry about any enemies I may make," Ponce said with a laugh. Then his face grew sober. "Gold and pearls—I should not reject them if they came my way. But I have never had wealth, and never missed it. It is not for the hope of treasure that I would go to the Indies."

"I know that well, my boy," Don Pedro said approvingly. "I have said as much to His Majesty. Here is an honest soldier, I told him, who will have no thought but the good of Spain. I know, for I have trained him from boyhood. I have led him on many a battlefield. Your Majesty can trust him, I said, as you could trust me. And to this I pledge my sacred word of honor."

"You said that, my lord?" Juan was deeply moved. Impulsively he took the old man's hand and kissed it. "Whatever His Majesty decides, I shall never forget this."

"I said nothing that was not true. I have watched you grow from a raw country boy into a noble knight, intelligent, brave, and always loyal. Our master has need of such men. He will need them especially in this new land, so far from Spain. See that you serve him well, Juan, and justify my faith in you. But you will. I know you will."

He paused, while Juan stammered out his gratitude.

"Don't thank me yet," Don Pedro warned. "It is not settled. The King is still making up his list. I cannot promise that your name will be on it. But I do advise you to put your affairs in order, and be ready to sail on short notice. You will not be kept long in suspense."

The word came only a week later. Captain Don Juan Ponce de León was ordered to recruit sixty men for the Indies service. He chose them from among the best of Don Pedro's retainers; tough, vigorous young veterans who had proved themselves against the Moors.

The rest of the voyagers were a mixed lot. No one of consequence had wanted to go with Columbus on his first voyage. On this second one, with its promise of untold wealth, everyone wanted to go. The Admiral had been persuaded to load his ships with gentlemen adventurers. Some of them wanted only to grab gold by the handful and come home to spend it. Others had visions of setting up estates, building castles, becoming the lords of New Spain. They had never worked, and did not mean to. That would be left to the simple natives.

Room was found for a few carpenters and stone masons, some farmers and some miners. There was one priest, a Benedictine monk named Brother Boyl. But on the whole, it was not a very well-selected group of colonists for a permanent settlement.

This second Columbus expedition sailed on September 25, 1493. On his first voyage, the Admiral had left forty men on the coast of Haiti, which he called Hispaniola. They had already begun building the first Spanish town when he sailed away.

Columbus expected to find a flourishing little village when he returned. He was so anxious to reach Hispaniola that he sailed past several unexplored islands on the way. He was finally compelled to stop at one of them to take on fresh drinking water.

The natives there received them kindly. The chief told the white men that his island was called Borinquen, or Boriquen. We know it now as

Puerto Rico. Juan Ponce de León, like the other sea-weary voyagers, found its pleasant shade and delicious fruits a welcome treat. He could not know that this charming tropic isle would become more truly home to him than the sun-baked plains of his native Aragon.

# The Painful Beginning

AFTER the brief delay at Puerto Rico, the expedition pressed on to Haiti. And there, instead of the new Spanish village they had expected, they found nothing but ruin. A few charred timbers marked the site of the houses. Not a man, white or red, came forth to greet them.

Columbus landed, and sent his soldiers scouring into the jungle. The natives fled before them. It was days before they found a few Indians brave enough to tell what had happened.

According to them, the Spaniards had quit work as soon as the Admiral's ship was out of sight. They had gone gold hunting instead.

There never was a great deal of natural gold on Haiti. The streams yielded a little in nuggets and gold dust. But most of the gold ornaments worn by the Indians had been traded for with natives of other islands. Some may have come from the mainland of South America, not yet known to the Spanish. These ornaments were old; treasured family or religious heirlooms. The colonists snatched all they could see, and demanded more. They also set the Indians to panning the streams and digging the ground for the precious metal.

The natives told fearful tales of their treatment by the white men. It was not only that they were worked unmercifully, prodded on with swords until they dropped from exhaustion. Nor that those who could produce no gold were beaten to death. Roaring drunk on ship's rum and palm wine, the settlers found amusement in games which outdid

Nero. There was target practice with live targets who did not long remain alive, and unspeakable torture of women and children. C419839

This, of course, is the Indians' story. The settlers' side was not told, and could not be. For the natives, banding together, had destroyed the settlement, killing some white men and driving the others into the jungle, where they died. Not one of them remained alive to contradict the charges brought against them.

There is no way of making certain that the charges were true. But there is one good reason for believing it. In their later dealings with the natives, some Spaniards of that time are known to have acted with inhuman cruelty. Their excuse was the same as the one the first settlers must have used. Indians were not Christians, and therefore need not be considered as human beings. They were animals. And animals, the Spaniards held, were put on earth for man's pleasure.

Christopher Columbus, on his first visit, had worked very hard to win the friendship of the Indians. He now had the difficult task of winning it back. He was not helped by the Spaniards who came along on the second expedition. They were furious at the natives for what had happened to the settlers. They demanded that the whole tribe be wiped out in punishment.

The Admiral pointed out that Their Majesties wished the natives to be Christianized, not murdered. If for nothing else, they must be saved to do the heavy labor the colony needed. He issued strict orders that the native peoples were to be treated with kindness. Those who disobeyed, he warned, would be sternly punished. So much for that. And now to get about their real business, the business of building a settlement.

Calling his Spaniards together, the Admiral laid down his plans. There was work to be done, and plenty of it. These Spanish gentlemen might not know how to build a house. They knew what a house ought to look like. They could stand over the Indians and see that a floor was properly laid; that the walls were all of the same height. If in doubt, they could call in the few carpenters and stone masons for advice. But there were not nearly enough of these to do the work alone. Everyone would have to do his share.

He let that sink in, and then went on. This first site was not a good one. The Admiral had decided

to move farther along the northern coast. Here he selected a spot with a good natural harbor. It was there that Isabella would rise, the first European city of the New World.

The enterprise went badly. The natives labored unwillingly, and the whites were sullen and rebellious. The Admiral's strictness only infuriated them. Who was he, anyway, to order them about? A foreigner, and a lowborn foreigner at that. The son of a humble weaver. The proud Spaniards put their heads together and concocted letters home, telling friends at court of how they were being oppressed by this upstart Italian.

Poor Columbus, a fine sailor and a great explorer, had little skill at ruling men. He met rebellion with force, using the soldiers under his command. Colonists who refused to work were beaten, imprisoned, and threatened with hanging.

This was well enough until some of the army officers joined in the revolt. The Admiral could no longer be sure that his orders were carried out. To add to his troubles, tropic fever swept the camp. Columbus himself was prostrated with it for several weeks. While he lay ill, a number of the colonists seized a ship and sailed back to Spain.

In spite of the difficulties, however, the town of Isabella slowly took shape. Once the public buildings were under way, the Admiral turned his attention to farming. Plenty of colonists volunteered for the new plantations. Safely away from his eagle eye, they spent their time lying in hammocks, drinking palm wine, and cursing the day they left Spain for this wilderness. The livestock died, the seed grain rotted, and the natives grew ever more wretched under harsh treatment.

Columbus was somewhat cheered in the summer of 1494, when a ship arrived from Spain. Aboard it was his younger brother Bartholomew. Here at least was one man he could depend upon. He made Bartholomew his second in command, which did not please the Spaniards.

In spite of all that the brothers could do, the situation grew steadily worse. Severe punishments only made the colonists more sullen and resentful. The Indians, once so friendly, were openly hostile. After three years had passed, Columbus decided to go back to Spain and ask the King to give him an army to maintain discipline.

He sailed with two ships in the spring of 1496. Two hundred homesick colonists insisted on crowding aboard. He did not want them, and he was afraid of what they might do, once they were at sea. After all, his first crew had threatened to throw him overboard. This present lot had far more reason to hate him. Wisely enough, he decided to take along a company of soldiers. The troop he chose was the one commanded by Captain Juan Ponce de León.

Life in the Indies had been a long way from the glorious adventure of Captain Juan's dreams. But he had done what he had to do, serving Columbus as faithfully as he had served his King. It seems likely that he welcomed the chance to end that service when the voyage ended. At any rate, he did not rejoin the Admiral for his third voyage. It would be six years before he returned to Haiti.

How he spent the six years is unknown. What is known, in every painful detail, is what those years did to Christopher Columbus. They were bitter years. The complaints of the colonists brought about his downfall. He was replaced as governor of the Indies by Bobadilla, who sent the proud Admiral home in chains. Queen Isabella released him, but she did not give him back the governorship.

The Admiral's enemy, Bobadilla, was no great

improvement as governor. Their Majesties were distressed at the lack of progress in the new colony. Very little treasure had reached Spain. Instead, there was a steady stream of complaints and accusations. The colonists were doing nothing but loafing and quarreling among themselves. King Ferdinand briskly decided it was time to make a new start.

He appointed a new governor, Don Nícolas de Ovando. Ovando was given the biggest fleet yet; thirty ships and twenty-five hundred people. The new governor, a nobleman of high degree, included a number of his aristocratic friends among the company. The first colonists had had to leave their families behind. But Ovando's friends were permitted to bring wives and children, personal servants, horses and hunting dogs. Luxurious quarters aboard ship were fitted up for them.

More than half the men of the Ovando expedition were soldiers. Among them was Captain Juan Ponce de León.

They sailed on February 13, 1502. This date marks the end of Captain Juan's life in Europe. From this day on, his fate and fortune lie in the New World.

# The Lady in Black

THE winter voyage was a rough one. Most of the passengers kept to their cabins. Captain Juan, who was never seasick, briskly took his exercise in such space as the deck allowed. Often, except for the crew, he had it to himself.

Then one day the lady in black appeared. She gave him a polite but distant "good day," and moved to a place at the rail. There she stood quietly, looking out to sea.

Captain Juan knew her tragic story. She was Doña Inez de la Torre, sister to one of the noblemen in Ovando's train. She had been bride and widow in a single week.

The wedding had been a gay affair, ending in a three-day tournament. The bridegroom had taken an active part. And on the final day, with all the guests looking on, he had broken his neck in a fall from his horse.

The stricken bride had retreated to a convent. Now, one year later, her brother had persuaded her to see what a change of scene might do to lighten her grief.

Captain Juan's acquaintance with the lovely young widow was of the slightest. Standing there with her back to him, she had plainly forgotten his presence. Now and then her lips moved in prayer. Sometimes she lifted her handkerchief to her eyes. But mostly she gazed blankly at the tossing waves, her face set in a mask of hopeless sorrow.

An hour went by, and still she stood, scarcely moving. Juan's kind heart was touched. He picked up a small cask and brought it over to her.

"A poor seat, my lady," he said with a bow,

"but will you not try it? It is more comfortable than standing."

"Thank you, no," she answered without turning.

Then, as he did not go, she added stiffly, "You are very kind, sir. But I prefer to be alone."

"I can see that," he said with unusual bluntness. "Unfortunately, you will find very little solitude where you are going."

Startled, she turned at last to face him.

"Where I am going?" she echoed. "I go to my brother's house."

"True. But your brother's house in Hispaniola will be very different from his castle in Spain. I do not know what building may have taken place lately. But when I lived there, my house was a grass hut. Work was being done on the church, the offices, and law courts. But we soldiers had to be satisfied with living as the natives did. My men had a great palm-leaf barrack shed. For me the Indians built a separate hut. Woven mats divided it into two rooms. One room was mine. The other was shared by my sergeant and two corporals. When the sergeant snored, I assure you I longed for solitude too."

He spoke as he would have spoken to a child he wished to cheer up. He was delighted to see that he had caught her interest. Without thinking, she sank down on the cask he had placed for her.

"You have been there before, Captain—Captain Ponce de León, isn't it? I know nothing at all of this place. My brother thought I should go, and I agreed. But he did not say we should live in grass huts!"

"And I do not say it, my lady. All this was six years ago. Much must have changed since I was here before. But for myself, I found the hut a very pleasant home. Cool, and fragrant from the dried grasses. I got used to eating my meals from a palm leaf instead of a plate. My bed was not a bed at all, but a woven net slung from the hut's posts. A hammock, the Indians call it. Very comfortable, when one gets used to it. I ate sitting on the ground. The natives have no notion of furniture, or dishes, or any of the things we are accustomed to."

"But how strange! Tell me more, Captain."

He talked on and on, pleased to see that for the moment at least she had forgotten her grief. They were both startled when the ship's gong summoned them to dinner.

Always before, Doña Inez had sat pale and silent at the big table, crumbling her bread, eating little. But today she startled the company by telling them that in Hispaniola one ate from palm leaves instead of plates. At their disbelieving looks, she appealed to Juan.

"Tell them it's true, Captain. And tell them about the beds that are really nets. And the fruits that taste like nothing we know."

Her brother gave Captain Juan an approving glance. He himself had tried in vain to rouse his young sister from her mourning. Now at last she had found something to interest her.

"Yes, Captain," he said heartily. "Do tell us. You are the only one among us who has seen our new home. Let us hear what it will be like."

Ponce de León was not ordinarily a great talker. But under their urging, he told them something of daily life in the islands as he remembered it.

Answering their questions, he marveled at their ignorance. All they knew of the Indies was that riches were to be found there. They expected to live as they had lived in Spain, with all the comforts they were used to. Any work to be done would be done by Indian slaves. It would be a tropical para-

dise, where a white man could grow rich without lifting a finger. Captain Juan thought to himself that they were in for a few surprises.

For the rest of the voyage, Juan and Doña Inez were much together. The change in the young widow was startling. Her hollow cheeks filled out; color came back to her face and sparkle to her eyes. Although sorrow had made her look older, she was no more than twenty. And very pretty, too, now that the shadows had lifted. Captain Juan, who had begun their friendship out of pity, soon found friendship and pity ripening into love.

One night Captain Juan paced around and around the deserted deck and did a little earnest thinking.

How, he asked himself, would a wife fit into his plans? This time, he was coming to the islands to stay. He would devote his first six months to army duty. After that, he meant to ask the governor to release him to civilian life. With the long record of military service behind him, such a request could hardly be refused.

And then? Well, then, like his shipmates, he meant to make his fortune here in the islands. But his way of doing it would be very different from theirs.

He had talked it all over with good old Don Pedro before he left. "I mean to rise in the world," the boy Juan had said long ago. Always he had seen that rise as a restoration of the family fortune. Once the Ponces had had castles, and lands, and wealth. If he could, he meant to bring it all back again.

If he could! The years had gone by, and what had he done? Oh, he had risen a long way from the beggar at the gate. He was a knight, a professional soldier with a fine reputation. His King trusted him. But as yet wealth had not come his way. It was high time he did something about it.

"I've thought it all out," he had told his patron. "The Indies is the place. Gold does not lie about the islands for the picking, as my countrymen believe. I have been there, and I know. But gold is not the only treasure. No one seems to have thought of agriculture. Yet the island soil is rich. Europe is a ready market for foodstuff of all kinds. The true wealth of the islands will be in the plantations."

"But you said the colonists tried that, and failed," Don Pedro objected.

"They did not even try!" Juan said scornfully. "They thought of their plantations as country estates, where the lord could spend his time hunting and playing games. I shall go about it in earnest. Study the soil and the seasons, work with my workers. And I'll have patience to wait. It is not necessary to grow rich overnight. I do not hope to come back next year with my pockets bulging. Indeed, if all goes as I hope, I shall not come back at all. It is a fair country, this New Spain of ours. I should be content to end my days there."

Don Pedro had nodded in thoughtful approval.

"It will not be easy. But you have never sought the easy way, my son. You have chosen well. I pray God may bless your undertaking."

"It will not be easy." The words echoed in Juan's mind as he paced the dark deck. He had realized that. Not easy for him, accustomed to the rough life of barrack and camp. And far less easy for a delicately bred young woman. Yet, somehow, he did not think that Doña Inez would shrink from hardships. With her at his side, they could only lead to final success.

As custom required, he spoke first to her brother. This was on the last day of the voyage.

"I have little to offer her, sir," he admitted. "Mine is a proud name, but there are neither estates nor fortune behind it. If God is good, I hope to remedy that here in the islands. For the present, I have only my heart to give her."

"A gift she longs for, if my eyes do not deceive me," the brother answered. "You have brought her back to life, Captain Juan. It is well and good that your lives should lie together. Tell her your marriage would have my blessing."

Captain Juan wasted no time. He went on deck, to find Inez in their favorite spot. The setting sun threw its last beams on her radiant face.

"Look!" she cried. "There on the horizon—it is, it must be the island. I can make out the palm trees, and the dark mountain behind it. It's like a vision of paradise! But what is it, Captain Juan? You look so sober. You do not smile. Are you not happy, then, to see your new home at last?"

"I should be happier," he said gently, "if I could think of it as *our* new home. I have spoken to your brother, Doña Inez. He says—"

"Oh, you spoke to him then?" she interrupted. "I told him if you didn't, he'd have to speak to you.

Oh, what have I said?" She blushed furiously, and hid her face in her hands.

Tenderly he pulled them away, and gathered her into his arms.

"You've said all that was needed to make me the happiest man in the New World," he told her. "Or in the Old one, for that matter. My darling little one, I shall see that you never regret it. We'll leave old sorrows, old heartaches behind. There, beyond the setting sun, lies our new life together. God send it be a happy one."

She looked up into his eyes. "I never thought to know happiness again, Juan. You have given it back to me. Between us, we will never let it go."

# The Adelantado

THERE had been changes on Haiti since Juan's first visit. Besides Isabella, there was a new town on the south coast, built by the Admiral's brother Bartholomew. It was at this new port of Santo Domingo that Ovando's expedition landed.

Bartholomew Columbus had built Santo Domingo in faithful imitation of a Spanish town. It had a central plaza, with the church and government buildings grouped around an open square. These buildings were of stone, roughly built, with roofs of palm thatch. Other houses were mostly of wood, plastered over with clay.

The governor's residence, called a palace, was hardly that. But it was the biggest and finest of the stone buildings. Ovando, the new governor, promptly moved into it and set up his court. He was the King's representative here. He meant to rule as royally as any king.

A king, of course, must have courtiers around him. Ovando's most favored friends were assigned the best houses in town. In addition, they were given vast country plantations, with Indian slaves to work them. The slaves were set to building "castles" for their masters to occupy when they visited their estates. It was not expected that the high nobles would live in the country. They would spend most of their time at the palace, as was the custom of Spanish nobles at home. Overseers would run the estates, keeping the slaves busy tilling the soil and digging gold.

Captain Juan had a different idea of plantation life. He had no chance to put it into practice. To his disappointment, Ovando refused his request for land.

"Later, perhaps," the governor promised him. "For the present, I cannot spare you from my army. From all I hear, these native workers are troublesome. They must be made to know, once for all, that we are their masters. Until they are broken to complete submission, my soldiers will have no time for farming."

Juan had no choice but to obey. He and Doña Inez were married a few days after their arrival. His men were lodged in barracks on the plaza. He himself, as a married officer, was assigned a house nearby. It was not the grass hut of the early days, but it was a long way from the luxurious home his bride had known.

Doña Inez thought the change was for the better. She was young and strong, and discomfort did not bother her. She delighted in the beautiful island scenery. She was keenly interested in the native people, and in their ways of living. The Indians given her as house servants found her a kind and gracious mistress.

Queen Isabella had commanded that the natives

were to be taught the Christian religion by their masters. Inez and her husband were among the few settlers who took this command seriously. Most of the newcomers were interested only in getting the last ounce of work out of their slaves. They cared little for Indian souls, and less for Indian bodies.

Governor Ovando himself set a poor example. It suited him better to have the natives remain heathen. Heathens had no rights. They were work animals, to be flogged mercilessly through their tasks, to be fed just enough to keep them alive. If they died, they could be replaced by others.

They did die, in frightening numbers. Starvation and backbreaking toil reduced them to a pitiful remnant. Those who still lived watched their chances and ran away. The plantation owners began to pester the governor with angry complaints. What good was a plantation, without enough men to work it?

Ovando responded by sending soldiers into the jungle to bring back the runaways. He supplied hunting dogs to make the task easier. The terrified Indians were chased through swamps and forests. Many of them were overtaken and brought back. Governor Ovando ordered their right legs broken

so they could not run away again. A broken leg does not help a sick and starving man to work better. The death rate on the plantations went up. The owners came back with new complaints.

The governor found a new remedy. Again he sent his soldiers forth. This time they were to go to the distant parts of the island, where white men had never been. They were to subdue the tribes there, and bring back new slaves.

This they did, and the old story started all over again. The new men were worked to death. When they died, the army was sent out for more.

Captain Juan Ponce de León led his company on these slave-hunting expeditions. Whatever he may have felt, he did not protest this cruel duty. He was an army officer under the governor's orders. He was not asked to approve those orders. A soldier's first duty was to obey. So Don Pedro had taught him. Loyal service to his superiors was Ponce's pride. He was ordered to hunt slaves and he hunted them, as skilfully and fiercely as he had fought the Moors.

He did especially well at it in the southeastern province of Higuey. The wild tribesmen there fought a bitter war before they were brought to submission. Most of the able-bodied men were sent back to Santo Domingo to work the plantations there.

Higuey itself proved to be fertile country, suitable for settlement. As a reward for his services, Ovando made Juan subgovernor, or *Adelantado*, of the region. He was given a huge plantation of his own, and complete authority to rule in Ovando's name. He would be short of workers at first, until the young boys grew up or the wounded warriors recovered. But that was his problem.

Captain Juan gladly acecpted his task. For the first time now he was free to deal with the natives in his own way. His true self shows plainly in the first thing he did.

The fighting had left scores of helplessly wounded Indians scattered through the forest. Ponce de León commanded them to be brought to a camp he had set up in a clearing. There their wounds were washed, broken bones set, bullets extracted. Those who could walk were fed and sent home. The others were allowed to have their families come to them.

Word spread among the Indians that this white lord was different from the others. They found they could bring their complaints to him and receive justice, even if it meant stern punishment for a Spanish soldier. Bit by bit they learned to trust him.

Doña Inez joined her husband soon after peace was restored. She was of great help in winning the confidence of the Indians. She went among the women, collecting cooking recipes, learning their language and customs. When she tried nursing at the hospital camp, she found that some of the old women knew more about it than she did. She got them to show her the native plants they used for medicine, and the ways they prepared them.

While she worked with the Indian women, Doña Inez talked gently of God the Father, of Our Lady and Her little Son, of the soul and its salvation. More than a year passed before Ovando heeded her plea and sent them a priest. When he arrived, he found an astonishing number of converts, already well instructed and ready for baptism.

# Plantation Life

CAPTAIN Juan and his wife had four peaceful, pleasant years in Higuey. A little
daughter, Isabel, was born in their new house on a
hill called Alta Gracia. The house was inside the
fort, for Juan was still a military commander. But
he was a civil ruler too, and he ruled mildly and
kindly.

Outside the fort lay the fields of his plantation.
Other followers of Ovando had asked for Higuey

land, but they found it very disappointing. What they wanted was gold. Once they realized there was no gold here, most of them went back to the gayer life of Santo Domingo. This suited Captain Juan very well. Left to himself, he developed his farming lands according to his own ideas.

A good part of it was set aside as pasture for cattle. The meat, pickled in brine, was shipped to Spain, where it brought high prices. But even more important were the products of the cultivated fields.

His principal crops were corn and sugar cane. Corn, which the Indians called maize, was native to the New World. Sugar cane had first been brought by Columbus from the Canary Islands. It grew even better in the isles of the west. And it became Juan's greatest source of income. The European countries were not so fond of sugar, but they did like rum, made from the fermented juice.

Unlike the other Spaniards, Captain Juan kept the management of his plantation in his own hands. He sent to Spain for a few experienced farmers, and the latest tools. They taught the natives what they knew, and in return were taught by them. The

Indians' only plow was a crooked stick, but they were wise in the ways of weather and soil. As best he could, Juan attempted scientific farming. It was very crude by present-day standards, but far in advance of his time. It paid him by yielding a rich return.

The plantation labor, of course, was done by native Indians. These workers were more like share croppers than slaves. They were paid in the grain and meat they produced. Well fed and kindly treated, they labored willingly. Captain Juan had no need of soldiers to keep his workers from running away.

He might have been content to live out his life on his Haitian plantation. But the whole course of his life was changed one day by a chance visitor.

From the windows of his house on Alta Gracia, Juan could see the green island of Borinquen, or Puerto Rico. He had visited it once, on his trip with Columbus. Other Spaniards had touched it briefly, to take on drinking water. It had never been thoroughly explored.

One summer afternoon a strange Indian paddled

his canoe across the fifty-mile channel between Haiti and Puerto Rico. He asked to be taken to the *Adelantado*. Ponce de León received him courteously, and listened to his story.

The man came, he said, from Borinquen. His people had heard that the white men had many strange and wonderful things. Metal hooks to catch fish, axes to chop firewood. And most wonderful of all, tiny bells that made sweet music when worn as necklaces.

"I do not know if these stories are true," the visitor said. "But I should like very much to own a string of those bells. I do not come to beg," he added proudly. "We hear that the white men like yellow pebbles. I have brought some pebbles to trade for bells, if you have any."

"We have bells," Ponce de León answered. "Let me see your pebbles."

The man untied a net he had knotted around his neck. From it he poured three or four small gold nuggets.

"We find them in the beds of our streams," he explained. "They are not as pretty as bells, and they make no music. But if the white chief wants them, they are his."

"And the bells are yours," Ponce de León answered.

He motioned to his servant, who brought a string of small bells. These were used in Spain to keep track of the hunting hawks. Of all the trinkets the Spaniards brought with them, these hawks' bells were most popular with the island natives.

"You will stay awhile as my guest," Juan told the man after he had been thanked. "My servant will see that you have food and lodging."

As soon as the man had been led away, the officers around Juan began an eager clamor. They had found garrison life in this peaceful province very tiresome. The sight of gold excited them.

They were all for organizing an expedition and setting forth for Puerto Rico.

"A good strong force," they argued, "in case these heathen dare to resist us. We'll kill enough of them to show we mean business, and then set the rest to digging gold. It'll make all our fortunes!"

"I must think about it," Ponce de León said, and dismissed them. It was with a heavy heart that he talked to his wife that evening.

"I thought it was all behind me," he said sadly. "The killing, the cruelty, the senseless slaughter of these poor creatures who have done us no harm! Yet what can I do? Now that we know there is gold on Borinquen, Spain must have it. Ovando wants it, our royal master wants it—to say nothing of my greedy officers! If I do not go for it, someone else will. And the killing will begin all over again."

"Must there be killing?" she asked timidly. "The man who came today was happy to exchange his gold for hawks' bells. We have many things his people want. Could you not trade for the gold without fighting? That seems to me the sensible way. And the Christian way, too," she added.

"Sensible, and Christian—oh, I agree, my dear! But you saw how our countrymen behaved in Santo Domingo. Would you call their dealings with the natives sensible or Christian? Once they are let loose on Borinquen, it will be no different. And it is I who must lead them there. If only—wait! I have thought of a plan. Listen, and see what you think of it."

Doña Inez listened, and thought very well of it. The next day, Captain Juan unfolded it to his officers.

"We do not know if there is enough gold to be worth-while," he told them. "Before I lead an expedition to Borinquen, I must satisfy myself about that. Therefore, I am going back with this native. I shall take only a half-dozen men-at-arms with me. If we find the island is worth conquering, I will so report to Governor Ovando. He can then take what action he sees fit."

The officers grumbled, but there was nothing they could do. A few days later, Juan Ponce de León set out in a single small sailboat. Two sailors and six common soldiers, with the Indian from Borinquen, were his only companions.

Sailing by moonlight, they crossed the channel and reached the opposite shore at daybreak. The time was the late summer of 1508.

# The Meeting with Guaybana

HALTING his party on the shore, Ponce de
León sent the Puerto Rican Indian on ahead.
"Tell your chief that the *Adelantado* of Higuey
asks the honor of an audience with him," he said.
"Say that I come in peace, and that I bring many
gifts."

The man hurried off. The Spaniards were kept
waiting for most of the morning. Captain Juan

passed the time in preparation. He put on his finest shirt, his velvet doublet, and his long silk hose. Over them went greaves and corselet of shining steel. With his polished helmet, gauntlets, and jeweled sword, he might have appeared with pride at the Spanish court.

Like their captain, the soldiers had worn their oldest clothes for the rough channel crossing. Now they too put on their armor. Juan inspected them carefully, ordering one man to wash his face and another to scour his rusty pike with sand.

The sun was high when the guide returned. His master, Chief Guaybana, was ready to receive them. He led the way up a hill, and into a forest clearing. Captain Juan and his men marched smartly in military formation, followed by the two sailors carrying a heavy chest.

It was plain that Chief Guaybana also had prepared for this meeting. He lay in his hammock under a giant silk-cotton tree, with his court drawn up behind him. His youngest wives were fanning him with palm leaves. The older ones knelt, holding trays of fruit and wine. Behind them were the old men and the children. And all around, in an outer half-circle, stood ranks of stalwart warriors, their spears held at the ready.

Captain Juan halted at the edge of the clearing, while the messenger went forward. Kneeling respectfully, the guide informed his king that the visitors awaited his pleasure.

Without haste, Guaybana rose from his hammock and beckoned them nearer.

"You come in peace, white lord?" he asked.

"In peace, O King," Juan answered gravely, with his deepest bow. He straightened, and looked fearlessly into the chief's face.

For a long minute the two men studied each other. They were an impressive pair. Guaybana had no royal robes or shining armor. His only garment was a twist of cotton cloth; his neck, arms, and ankles circled with strings of sea shells. But broad muscles rippled under the copper skin. He held himself as proudly as any Spanish grandee.

The chief, for his part, saw a man as tall and broad-shouldered as himself. Honest friendly eyes looked out of a bronzed soldierly face.

Juan had put himself completely into the chief's power. One order to the waiting warriors, and the little handful of white men would be wiped out. But Guaybana's glance searched in vain for a hint of fear. His distrust melted before Juan's friendly gaze.

"You are welcome," he said at last. He gestured to his followers, and led the way into his hut.

The hut was a large, airy place, but it was a small party which sat down to the feast. Juan's soldiers were entertained by the villagers outside. Besides the chief, only three or four old counselors took their places on the heaps of palm leaves. There was also, to the captain's surprise, one woman. Usually, Indian women did not eat with their men. But the chief explained that this lady was his mother, whose great age and wisdom had earned her the privilege.

When they were seated, the wives entered, bearing immense leaves for plates. On them were heaped pineapples, berries, alligator pears, broiled fish and lizard, roast wild pig and yams. Calabashes held cocoanut milk or palm wine, and there was a particularly nasty kind of greenish beer. As politeness demanded, Juan ate and drank and praised everything offered him.

Guaybana and his counselors had many questions to ask. There was a little language difficulty,

but not much. The speech of all the island Indians was much like that of Haiti, which Juan had learned perfectly. It was only once in a while that he had to resort to the sign language here.

He answered their questions frankly, and he could feel their friendliness growing. Juan knew that he was accepted when Guaybana proposed that they exchange names. This was the natives' highest token of friendship. By it, the two men became brothers.

"Juan Ponce de León—my new name pleases me," the chief declared. "As I hope yours pleases you, Brother Guaybana."

"It pleases me very well," Juan answered. He lifted his wine cup. "May we live in peace, as brothers should. To peace and friendship, Brother Ponce!"

The Spanish custom of the toast had to be explained. Guaybana and his friends found it very agreeable. A number of toasts were drunk before the party returned to the clearing.

There Juan presented his offerings. The chest carried by the sailors held knives, fishhooks, hammers and axes, colored cloth, and a generous supply of hawks' bells. After Guaybana had made his choice, the remaining gifts were distributed among the delighted villagers.

In the hubbub of talk, the queen mother approached Captain Juan. She had said no word during dinner, but had studied him sharply with her keen old eyes. Now it seemed that she too was ready to show her approval.

She drew him a little apart, to where a young girl stood alone. "My daughter Atala," the old lady said. "I give her to you for your wife."

Captain Juan stood in embarrassed silence. The child, for she was scarcely more, waited with downcast eyes. She was very lovely in her scanty cotton petticoat and strings of shells, her long black hair covering her like a mantle.

Ponce de León cleared his throat. "You are most kind, madam," he said awkwardly. "But this is not a gift I could accept. I already have a wife."

"She does not please you?" the old woman said angrily. "You reject the chief's sister, white lord?"

He realized that this could be serious. Gently and patiently he began to explain. It was well known that different peoples had different customs. Among his people, it was not the custom to have more than one wife. Their laws forbade it. He would be breaking the law of his tribe if he took a second wife.

The queen mother listened with a frown. It was plain that she was not convinced. Then Captain Juan had an inspiration.

"I have a wife, your highness, but I have no sister. Your son has done me the honor to make me his brother. Would you permit me to make this young lady my sister? I would do it by the custom of my people. See, I would do it in this way."

From his neck he slipped a gold chain bearing a tiny gold cross. It had been Inez's wedding gift to him. Now he solemnly clasped it around the maiden's neck. She fingered it in shy pleasure, and her mother's face broke into smiles.

"Sister to the white lord! That is indeed an honor. See that you are worthy of it, my girl!"

She reached out her clawlike hands to examine the cross, and the other women crowded closer to see. Under cover of their chatter, Ponce de León thankfully made his way back to the group around the chief.

At the first opportunity, he turned the conversation to the "yellow pebbles." His countrymen valued them above all things, he told Guaybana. His

Indian guide had said they were to be found in the rivers of the island. Would the chief show him those rivers?

Guaybana frowned. Hunting pebbles, in his opinion, was a poor pastime for two mighty lords. The island was large. There were many rivers. There were also many chiefs, some of them his enemies. Better to stay here, in his own village, and have another feast.

As politely as he could, Juan tried to insist. Guaybana still refused to lower his dignity by going pebble hunting. Finally, however, he suggested something else. He would take his new friend on a real hunting trip, for wild pig. That was a fine sport, and pig meat was something worth having.

Captain Juan had to agree. The three-day hunting trip gave him at least a glimpse of the gold-bearing rivers. His followers managed to pick up a fair supply of nuggets and gold dust. With these, and with generous gifts of fruits and bone ornaments, he took ship for home.

# Juan Goes Exploring

BACK in Haiti, Captain Juan went at once to the capital city. There he displayed the gold to Governor Ovando, and described his visit to Borinquen.

"It is a fair and fertile land," he reported. "Guaybana's people are good farmers, too. I saw fields of corn and yucca stretching for many acres. I am certain other crops would grow there."

"Fields—crops!" the governor snorted. "What

do I care for those? It's the gold, man, the gold! You say this savage refused to show you the sources?"

"It was not that he refused, sir. He simply could not understand why we should waste our time poking about in river beds for pebbles. He thought hunting wild pig was a much better sport to offer me."

"A thin excuse!" Ovando said angrily. "The trouble with you, Ponce, is that you believe what these lying natives tell you. The fact is that he refused to show you where the gold comes from. You've admitted it. Well, we'll know how to deal with him. Force—that's the only thing these heathen understand. How many soldiers will you need to conquer the island?"

Ponce de León sighed. He saw no reason why Puerto Rico should be "conquered." The rich island was well worth having. He did not question that it must come under the control of Spain. But could it not be done in a peaceful manner? He thought he could do it in that manner, if he were left to himself. At least he would like to try.

He knew better than to make such a suggestion to the governor. Instead he said, cautiously, "It would be well to know more of the island before we invade it. My idea would be to make another peaceful visit first. This time I would take some miners, who can judge how rich the gold supply is. Also, I would survey the island, finding the best harbor, locating a spot for a fort. Once this is done, it will be far simpler to take possession."

Ovando looked at him admiringly. "You have a good head on your shoulders, Captain—I've always said that. Very well, it shall be as you say. But I'll give you a company of soldiers, just to make sure those heathen try no tricks."

Captain Juan spent a few weeks getting his expedition together. He selected his miners and map makers very carefully, but as to the soldiers he had no choice. They were from his garrison in Higuey. Their officers were the men who had been so anxious to go to Puerto Rico for gold. Like the governor, they talked disdainfully of the savages who must be made to turn over the treasure or take the consequences.

Ponce de León was prayerfully anxious to conclude his mission without bloodshed. The presence of so many armed men would be sure to alarm Guaybana and his people. How could he convince them that he came in peace? He could think of only one way. He decided to take his wife and child with him. This surely would prove that his intentions were peaceful. He himself had so deep a trust in Guaybana that he did not hesitate to put his dear ones in the chief's power.

Once again Captain Juan sailed across the channel. This time he had sixty common soldiers with him, four officers, and twenty civilians.

The chief and his people received them as kindly as before. The queen mother and her daughter were delighted with Doña Inez and the little girl. Juan's "sister" made herself the child's special guardian. Doña Inez, explaining the meaning of the gold cross, made her first Puerto Rican convert in the gentle Indian princess.

Juan left his family in the chief's village and set out to explore the island in earnest. Guaybana, still puzzled over the white men's interest in yellow pebbles, made no objection. He did not go himself, but he sent his younger brother Agueybana as guide. He furnished also a number of men as burden-bearers.

The route led them out of Guaybana's territory and into land held by lesser chiefs. As Guaybana had warned, some of these were his enemies. However, the strange chiefs were friendly enough to Juan. It may be that the strength of his armed following was responsible for this.

On the surface, the journey proceeded without incident. But all was not quite so serene as it seemed. Agueybana, the guide, was very different from his brother. He was a sullen, touchy young man, suspicious of strangers.

The Spanish soldiers gave him good ground for his suspicions. In spite of Juan's strict orders, they acted toward the natives as they had always acted. Heavy loads were heaped upon the carriers. If they faltered, they were urged on with kicks and curses. In the inland villages where they camped at night, the Spaniards were insolent and overbearing toward their hosts.

Agueybana was too proud to complain to Ponce de León, and the natives were too timid. Busy with his miners and surveyors, he did not see all that was going on. He saw enough to worry him, but there was not much he could do.

Compared with the early settlers on Santo Domingo, the men were behaving very well. No one had been killed or seriously hurt when the ex-

pedition ended. Ponce de León had to be satisfied with that. Young Agueybana was not satisfied at all. It was a bitter enemy that Juan left behind when he sailed again for Haiti.

He left his wife and child in the queen mother's care. This absence would be a short one. He would report his findings to Ovando, and return with settlers for a permanent colony. With any luck at all, he hoped to be made governor of the new territory.

# The Conquest of Puerto Rico

JUAN reached Santo Domingo, all unsuspect-
ing, to find the capital city decked with
flowers and banners. A week-long *fiesta* was just
ending. What was it all about? Why, didn't he
know? To welcome the new governor, of course.

A few more questions ended his puzzlement. His
friend Ovando, it appeared, had been recalled to
Spain. In his place, the islands had a new governor
with a famous name.

This was Don Diego Columbus, son of Christopher. The old Admiral was dead now, but his son had successfully pressed his claim against Spain. Christopher Columbus had been promised that he should rule all the Western possessions. Although his enemies had overthrown him, the royal promise still stood. Diego had claimed and received the post which had been taken from his father.

Don Diego had no love for Ovando, nor for any friends of his. He listened greedily to Juan's account of Puerto Rico. The island must come under Spanish rule without delay. Any talk of friendly settlement was nonsense. One did not make friends with savages. His distinguished father had thought otherwise. But Don Diego, brought up in Spain, had the Spanish view. Conquest by fire and sword, that was the good old Spanish way. He would send out a Puerto Rican expedition at once.

Juan was not even considered as leader. The governor appointed two followers of his own, Juan Cerón and Miguel Díaz. They would choose their own officers, Captain Juan was coldly informed. Neither of them chose him.

Ponce de León spent all night wrestling with that fierce pride of his. War was coming to Puerto

Rico, and his wife and child were there. At any cost, he must get back to the island. Since there was no other way, he humiliated himself and joined the new army as a common soldier.

Cerón and Díaz landed as an invading force. They announced their intentions by setting fire to Guaybana's village. The terrified Indians fled into the hills, taking Inez and little Isabel with them.

In the next few months, the Spaniards spread out across the land, seeking gold in the river beds. Wherever they found it, they raided the villages for slaves to dig it out. The natives, not yet organized for war, put up little resistance, although there were some bloody skirmishes. Always the white men prevailed, burning villages and killing the inhabitants as a lesson to the others.

While this was going on, Ovando was back in Spain, pulling all the wires he could. He did not succeed in doing much for himself, but he did put in a word for Ponce de León. Juan's good friend Don Pedro added his persuasions. Between them, they convinced His Majesty that he could not afford to lose this brave and loyal officer.

King Ferdinand sent a message to Governor

Diego Columbus. Cerón and Díaz were to be re-
lieved of their command. Conquest of the island
would be completed by Captain Juan Ponce de
León, whom the King was appointing as Puerto
Rico's governor.

This was the sense of the message, although the
King did not put it so bluntly. He had given Diego
Columbus full authority to rule all the islands. It
was for Don Diego to choose commanders and ap-
point subgovernors. But when His Majesty ex-
pressed a desire to see certain steps taken, Diego
hurried to take them.

In any case, he had not been too satisfied with
the slow course of events in Puerto Rico. Very little
gold had trickled back to Haiti. He complied willingly with the King's suggestions. Notifying Ponce
de León of his appointment, he sent along a new
army. It was His Majesty's will and his own, Don
Diego wrote pompously, that the new governor
complete the conquest in short order.

Juan still had hopes that the conquest could be
accomplished peacefully. He was soon undeceived.

Now in command, he advanced upon the village
to which Guaybana had fled. He found his wife
and daughter safe with the queen mother and a

handful of women. There was not an able-bodied man in the camp.

Tearfully the old lady told him her sad news. Her son Guaybana was dead—at whose hands she could not or would not say. Doña Inez told her husband that the women suspected it was his brother's hand which had struck the blow.

At any rate, Guaybana was dead, and Agueybana reigned in his stead. The young chief was now in the interior, raising a mighty force among all the island tribes. They had forgotten old enmities and united under his leadership. With him they had sworn to rid the island of the invaders, leaving no white man alive.

The Spaniards had already started building a fort at a place called Caparra. Juan took his family there, urging the old queen and her daughter to come along. They proudly refused. Whatever came, their place was with their people.

What came was a full scale war between the whites and Agueybana. It raged for nearly two years until Agueybana was killed and his forces surrendered.

No one knows what happened to Guaybana's mother and sister. Juan tried very hard to find some trace of them, but failed. A year after the war ended, he saw the little gold cross on a soldier's neck. The man said he had won it from another soldier in a dice game. No, he did not know the man, and he had not heard how the cross came into his possession.

Juan bought it from him and gave it to his daughter. Isabel wore it to the day of her death. It was all that remained to remind them of the Indian girl who had been Puerto Rico's first Christian.

# Lord of Borinquen

AS *Adelantado* of Higuey, Captain Juan had had the task of getting a ruined region back on its feet. He was *Adelantado* of Puerto Rico now, and he had the same job on a bigger scale. Puerto Rico was far larger than the Haitian province. The two-year war had left it in far worse shape.

Both Diego Columbus in Haiti and the King in Spain were expecting gold from the new possession. Juan's explorations had already convinced him that there was not a great deal of gold in the Puerto Rican streams. As a matter of fact, none of the Caribbean islands ever yielded enough gold to satisfy Spain. It was not until later, with the conquest of Mexico and Peru, that the golden stream really began to flow to the mother country.

Ponce de León put his miners to work digging out what gold there was. Native divers brought up a scanty supply of pearls from the lagoons. But again, as in Haiti, agriculture offered the best source of wealth.

This disappointed Don Diego, but it suited Ponce de León very well. The soil here was even richer than that of his plantation in Higuey. It proved especially good for growing sugar cane. Captain Juan, bringing sugar cane to Puerto Rico, gave it what has been the island's principal crop from his day to our own.

He had two years as royal governor of Puerto Rico. In that time, from 1510 to 1512, he transformed it into a flourishing Spanish province. Several towns were built, among them the city of San Juan which still remains the capital. He built it as a European-style walled town, with a fort and military barracks.

One of the most imposing buildings was his own home, a stone castle called Casa Blanca (White House). Visitors to San Juan are shown a Casa Blanca still standing. Some guidebooks maintain that this is the original house. However, historians agree that Juan's son Luis tore down the old house after his father's death and built a new and bigger Casa Blanca.

The orginal Casa Blanca was new enough and big enough to impress all who saw it. At last Juan could give Doña Inez the luxury she deserved. The castle's furniture, mostly made by native craftsmen, was of the rare woods in which the island abounded. Fine tapestries and carpets, imported from Spain, softened the stone walls and floors. Irish damask, Venetian crystal, Dutch silver adorned the table. Hundreds of wax candles in silver holders lighted the great hall, where minstrels entertained Doña Inez's guests.

Besides his city castle, Ponce de León had a more modest but still luxurious house on his country plantation. A stone-paved road led to it. The road was especially wide to accommodate the Ponce de León carriage, the first wheeled vehicle ever seen in Puerto Rico.

All this gracious living cost money, a great deal of it. But money was coming in from the sale of cattle and grain, from the rum distilleries of the plantation. Captain Juan spent it recklessly. No doubt he would have been wiser to save some of it against a rainy day.

The rainy day came just a year after he and Doña Inez had settled into Casa Blanca. They were celebrating the birth of Luis, their second child. The rejoicings were interrupted by the arrival of a boat from Haiti. It carried his old enemies, Cerón and Díaz.

Juan's treatment of these two men had not been wise. His pride had suffered from having to serve under them as a private soldier. When he was ordered to replace them, he repaid old affronts by sending them back to Spain as prisoners. He had no authority to do this, and the King was not pleased. Diego Columbus, who had chosen them in the first place, was furious when he heard the news. He chose to take it as a personal insult, and wrote the King indignant letters about it.

King Ferdinand's position on island affairs was always difficult. He had no way of knowing what was going on except through what he was told. He was told a good many things, not always strictly true. He liked and trusted Captain Juan. But after all, he had made Diego Columbus Overlord of all the Indies. If Don Diego objected to a governor under him, it seemed right to yield to his objections.

So, after the matter had simmered for two years, King Ferdinand acted again. Cerón and Díaz were reinstated as governors of Puerto Rico. However, the King expressly commanded that Ponce de León was to be treated with respect, and allowed to keep all personal property. This included Casa Blanca, which he had built at his own expense, and his vast plantations.

Juan was bitterly unhappy at having to surrender his post. He thought, with reason, that he had made a very good governor. He doubted whether the two men would do as well. He wrote his old friend Don Pedro to urge the King to give him back the office. Don Pedro and other friends did their best, but nothing came of it.

As a gentleman of leisure, Juan could give all his time to his plantations now. He worked out an improved process for distilling rum, and the money poured in almost as lavishly as ever. The family spent most of their time in the country now. Their

third child was born there. Most men would have been content with the peaceful, prosperous life of a country gentleman.

Juan Ponce de León was far from content. His life had been passed in the service of his King. First as soldier, then as governor of the Haitian province and then of Puerto Rico, he had put duty to his country first. Now, all at once, he had no duty to anyone but himself and his family. It was not so that he had expected to end his days. He had grown used to ruling men, to a position of authority. He could not resign himself to giving it all up.

He was restless and uneasy, ready to grasp at anything that would bring him back to public life. The opportunity came in a strange form, just when he least expected it.

# The Fountain of Youth

ONE day an Indian woman came to Casa Blanca, asking to see the master. She was very old, and very tired. She had walked a long way, day and night, from her home in the far mountains. She refused to tell her business to anyone but the white lord.

Captain Juan told the guards to bring her in. At first glance, he could see that she was near fainting from exhaustion. He had food and drink brought for her, and told her kindly to take her time.

She ate greedily, and then began her story. She was a Carib, from the island of Guadeloupe. Some years before, her tribe had come to settle in the Puerto Rico hills. Later, her husband and his brothers had taken their biggest canoe and paddled away, leaving her behind.

No, they were not going home to Guadeloupe, she went on. They were bound for Bimini, land of the magic Fountain of Youth. Her husband was an old man hoping to grow young again. He had promised to come back for his wife and take her to Bimini.

"But the years go by, and he does not come," she said tearfully. "I grow old and ugly, your grace. He has grown young again, and he forgets his old wife. But if I can reach that place and bathe in the waters, I will be once again the young girl he married. You also, your grace," she added artfully, "would bene-fit from the magic waters. With respect, one sees that you are no longer a youth. You have many ships. It would be a small matter for you to take me to Bimini. And your lordship would not be the loser by doing a poor old woman a favor."

Ponce de León looked surprised. This was not the first time he had heard of the fabled fountain of Bimini. Many Indians on Haiti and Puerto Rico swore that it existed. The trouble was, no one knew where Bimini might be. It could be any one of the hundreds of unexplored islands of the West Indies. So far, the Spanish had visited and settled only a few of the larger ones. All else was unknown territory.

"You could find the way to Bimini?" he asked now. "Have you been there, then?"

No, she had not been there, she admitted. Nor had any of her people. But she had heard her husband and his brothers plan their route. She knew exactly the direction they meant to take, the landmarks that would guide them.

When Ponce de León asked shrewdly how *they* knew, she grew a little confused. All she could say was that her husband was a very wise man. He knew many things that he did not tell his wife.

"Your grace need have no fear," she said positively. "I can lead you to the island. If the fountain does not attract you, there is much gold to be found there. And pearls, of course. My people do not value these things, but I know the white lords cherish them. The treasures are yours to take. For myself, I ask only to find my husband, and to bathe in the magic waters."

"And you are certain you could guide me to Bimini?" Ponce de León asked again.

She was quite certain. If she failed, they might take her life. For life indeed meant nothing to her unless she could find her lost husband.

Captain Juan promised to think it over. *La Vieja*, the Old One, as the Spaniards called her, was given lodging at Casa Blanca, while Ponce de León took counsel with his officers.

Everyone was eager to make the expedition. Some of them believed wholeheartedly in the magic fountain. They pointed out that the Indians did possess herbs which stopped bleeding and reduced fever. These medicines would have seemed magic in Europe, where they were unknown. Why might not the waters of this unknown fountain also have unheard-of powers?

One young fellow stumbled upon a new argument. He himself had no need to grow younger. But Ferdinand, their gracious King, was a sick man, and an aging one. What would His Majesty not give for a cask of this water, if they could find it?

For that matter, what would not any elderly nobleman give? Why, a single shipload of barreled water would be worth all the gold of the Indies! And they, the discoverers, could set their own price.

Captain Juan listened in thoughtful silence. He was too hardheaded to place much faith in the old woman's story. That she believed it herself he had no doubt. But she had not seen the fountain. She had not even seen the island of Bimini. In her eagerness to search for her husband, she was promising everything—youth-giving waters, gold, pearls. There was no way of knowing whether she could keep these promises.

Yes, there was a way. One could go and see. He was his own man now, with no governor's duties to distract him. That thought brought another one. Once before he had followed a strange Indian guide. That step had led to his exploring and conquering Puerto Rico. It had led him to a governorship. Could it happen again? Bimini was new territory, as yet unclaimed for Spain. Governor of Bimini—why not?

Old ambitions flamed anew. Captain Juan wrote to the King, and to his friends at court. He asked for a royal grant to explore and settle the island of

Bimini, with the right to govern it as *Adelantado*. He promised to set aside for the crown the usual percentage of profit from all gold, pearls, and Indian slaves found there. His letter made no mention of magic water. Time enough to deal with that if it existed. If it did not, there was no use risking ridicule by seeming to believe in it.

How much Ponce de León did believe in it is anybody's guess. Some writers have pictured him as a decrepit old man, foolishly swallowing any tale that would promise to make him young again. The fact is that he was now fifty-three, a vigorous hard-bitten soldier as active as any young man under his command. He probably did think it would be pleasant to return to youth. Most middle-aged people think so. But nothing in his actions shows that renewing his own youth was the chief reason for the expedition.

The royal grant came a few months later. It provided for a higher share of royal profits than Juan had offered, and it was a little indefinite about the governorship. But in the main, it gave him the permission he had sought. It does not refer to the Fountain of Youth, as Juan's application had not mentioned it.

His Majesty may have heard some of the stories about the fountain which were circulating in the islands. If he did, he took no notice of them. It is not likely that they attracted too much attention even on Puerto Rico.

Juan did have offers from two elderly plantation owners to pay part of his expenses if they could go along as passengers. Their only reason for making the uncomfortable trip must have been the prospect of bathing in the magic waters.

Ponce de León politely refused the offers. He would pay for the voyage out of his own funds, and he would choose his own companions.

The companions he chose were mostly the sons of colonists, without land of their own. If they found good land for the taking on Bimini, they would be rewarded with plantations. They were well armed, and ready to fight if necessary, but he hoped it would not come to that. Captain Juan firmly believed that he could have settled Puerto Rico without bloodshed, if he had been allowed to use his own methods. He meant to give those methods a second trial on Bimini.

On March 3, 1513, Captain Juan bade farewell to his wife and children. With her son and two daughters, Doña Inez would remain at the plantation, seeing that all went well in the fields. She was a young woman still, twenty-five years younger than her husband. Did she hope to see him return a young man of her own age? We shall never know.

There were three ships in the expedition. Besides the old Indian woman who claimed to know the way, Captain Juan took along a famous pilot, Anton de Alaminos, who had served Columbus on his last voyage. *La Vieja* might know how to find Bimini, but she certainly could not be trusted to navigate a ship through the islands and reefs that lay along the way.

# The Discovery of Florida

SLOWLY the three ships made their way northwestward, through the chain of islands now known as the Bahamas.

There are nearly two thousand of these, some mere points of rocks sticking up from the sea. They were not entirely unknown to the Spanish. Some had been visited by slave hunters from Haiti. The

Bahamians were skilled divers, useful for pearl fishing. However, the Spanish visits had been brief raids, with no attempt at settlement.

Ponce de León made one stop in the Bahamas, at the island of San Salvador. This was the island where Columbus had made his first landing. It was nearly deserted now. Most of the natives had long since been carried off to work on Haiti. Captain Juan stayed for two or three days, making repairs to a ship which had sprung a leak. Then the voyage was resumed.

So far as the white men knew, any one of the Bahamas might have been Bimini. But the old woman who was their guide was very positive. Not here, not here, she declared of every isle they passed. Under her direction, they continued ever farther to the northwest, until at last the Bahamas were left behind.

They were out of sight of land for several days. Then on Easter Sunday, the 27th of March, the lookout sighted a low coast line lying to the west. *La Vieja* was summoned, and peered at it through the vast lifting mists. In great excitement, she announced that this was indeed Bimini.

Whether it was the long-sought island or not,

it offered no safe landing place at that point. Rocky reefs and sand bars lay between them and the land. To add to the difficulty, a storm blew up and swept them out to sea. The shore line disappeared in wind-driven rain.

They rode out the storm and turned again toward the west. For several days they coasted north, seeking a place to land. They found it sometime toward the week's end. The exact day is unknown. So also is the exact location of the landing place. It was somewhere near where the city of St. Augustine now stands.

Night was coming on when they anchored. The next morning, in the light of the rising sun, the adventurers had their first good look at the land.

The sight was unbelievably beautiful. Green waves rolled up to a silver beach of hard-packed shell. Behind it loomed a dense green forest of tulip trees and magnolias in full bloom. Low-growing azaleas and jasmine flowers seemed alive with hummingbirds and butterflies. The sweet scent of the blossoms drifted to sea, borne on a soft warm breeze.

Ponce de León and his men went ashore. Their first act was to plant the Spanish flag on the beach, and formally take possession in the name of the King.

The second was to give the new territory a proper Christian name. "Bimini" might do well enough for the heathen Indians, but Spanish land must be named in Spanish. Since it was the Easter season, and because of the blooms all around them, they called it *Pascua Florida*, Easter of Flowers.

The ceremonies over, they moved on to explore the thick woods behind the beach. They went cautiously, keeping their weapons ready, but they came upon no inhabitants. There were no trails in the heavy undergrowth, and no sign of a village. So far as they could tell, they were the only human beings in this earthly paradise.

They spent only a day or two at this first landing place. If any of the time was passed in searching for a magic fountain, the record does not show it. Certainly none was found. Far more disappointing, there were no signs of gold or pearls. Captain Juan's men readily agreed to take to the ships again and proceed further along the coast.

They tried to continue north. But bad weather and unfavorable currents forced them to turn south again. They passed their first landfall, and continued down the Florida coast. At some point, now unknown, they saw a cluster of Indian huts. As they came in closer, they could see a group of natives watching them from the beach.

Captain Juan's mind went back to his first visit to Puerto Rico. He had gone fearlessly ashore, accompanied only by a handful of men. The very fact that there were so few of them had convinced Chief Guaybana that his intentions were peaceful. Would these Florida Indians be impressed in the same way? He decided it was worth trying.

He took only one boatload of men and went ashore. To his disappointment, he found that these people did not understand any Indian language he knew. But they seemed friendly enough. By signs they invited the white men to sit down, and indicated that they would bring food. Then all of them disappeared among the trees.

Juan and his companions waited for some time, sitting in a half-circle on the warm sand. They were in the open, but quite close to a belt of trees. There was not an Indian in sight when all at once a rain of arrows darkened the air. Perched in the trees, the marksmen were invisible, while the white men made an easy target. As luck would have it, no one was hurt in the first volley. Ponce and his men did not wait for a second. Far outnumbered, they could do nothing but flee to their ship.

Some of the hotheads among his officers were for making another landing in force. Captain Juan, however, ruled against it. He had made an unfortunate beginning. Better to go on to a new spot, and a new group of natives. He still hoped that he could win good will by a display of presents, which he had had no chance to make here. All Indians, he reasoned, wanted knives and fishhooks and hawks' bells.

It took several sharp encounters to convince him that he was wrong. These Florida Indians wanted nothing that the white men had. They were as cunning as they were fierce. Several times Ponce and his men were led into traps, convinced that the natives were ready to trade. Every time the meeting ended in battle that forced the Spaniards to flight.

Ponce de León, a seasoned Indian fighter, does not come very gloriously out of these episodes. Fighting on this coast was different from the Indian fighting he had known. The natives could melt into their forests at will. They moved with ease through these trackless forests, where the Spaniards had to hack their way through the undergrowth. While they stumbled along, the Indians sent their darts whistling through innocent flowery branches overhead. Their numbers could not be guessed at. It seemed to the invaders that there must be hundreds waiting to take the place of every man who fell to a musket ball.

Captain Juan had to face the fact that he would need a real army to subdue this land. For the present, it seemed more important to find out whether it was worth conquering.

His men did not think it was. The absence of any treasure had dampened their enthusiasm. Flowers and fruits were all very well, but they put no money in a man's pockets. They urged their commander to press on along the coast, hoping for better luck.

Ponce de León was quite willing. What chiefly impressed him was the size of this island. That it was an island he had no doubt. No one yet knew that there was a North American continent of which Florida was a small part.

He thought it must be a very large island. Larger, perhaps, than Cuba, the biggest one the

Spanish had found so far. To be governor of a larger island than Cuba would be a very fine thing. Captain Juan was anxious to find out the size of his new territory. After that, he could come back again and set up his government.

They sailed all the way down to Florida's southern tip, and rounded it into the Gulf of Mexico. Then north again, following the coast line. A truly enormous island this must be! On and on they went, certainly as far as Apalachee Bay. They may have gone much farther.

At some point along the west coast they had their fiercest battle with the natives. This time they were attacked by a fleet of canoes, as well as a land force. The ships' cannons were able to disperse the eighty canoes, and to do some damage on the beach. After that, the Spanish ships found it prudent to move far out to sea.

Ponce de León was ready to go home. He had seen enough to satisfy him that he had made an important discovery. Whether Florida was rich in gold remained to be seen. He had never penetrated inland. From the coast, he could not tell whether there was open land for farming. But he thought there must be. Surely the trees could not cover the

entire island! And their luxuriant growth proved
that the soil was rich. He must get back to Puerto
Rico and arrange for a colonizing expedition.

They turned for home with the hearty approval
of all on board. All, that is, except one. *La Vieja*
was not happy about the result of the voyage. She
had not found the fountain. More important still,
she had not found her husband. Since her husband
and the fountain were certainly on Bimini, she
decided she had been mistaken. This island was not
Bimini, after all.

She hurried to tell Ponce de León of her con-
clusion. She knew now she had been wrong. Bimini
was farther out in the Atlantic, more to the east-
ward. She still wanted to go there. And now, having thought it all over, she was quite sure she could
find the right way.

Captain Juan heard her with good-natured impatience. Later, perhaps, when he came back again
to settle Florida. Time enough then to search all
the islands round about.

One of his captains was more sympathetic. Juan
Pérez de Ortubia was as unwilling as *La Vieja* to
give up the search for Bimini. At his urging,
Captain Juan agreed that Ortubia could take one

ship and follow the old woman's new directions.

The vessels separated in Biscayne Bay. Ponce de León and two ships went back to Puerto Rico, where they arrived on September 21, 1513.

Captain Ortubia came in a couple of weeks later. For what it was worth, he had found Bimini. At least, he had found an island with a fountain, if you could use that word for a natural spring leaping from a cliff.

There is an island called Bimini on our maps today. It may or may not be the one Ortubia visited. It lies between Nassau and Miami, a popular resort for big game fishermen. There is a yacht club there, and several modern hotels, but no Fountain of Youth.

There was certainly some sort of spring on the Bimini Captain Ortubia found. But unhappily, neither he nor his men came back any younger. They had given the fountain a fair trial, too. When the first hasty plunge showed no results, they had soaked themselves for hours. They had even tried drinking it. This was quite a sacrifice for the Spanish sailors, who usually quenched their thirst with wine or rum. Neither swallowing the stuff nor wallowing in it had worked a miracle. They were cleaner than they had ever been, per- haps, and that was all.

*La Vieja* was missing from the ship's company. It was whispered that Captain Ortubia thrust the old woman's head under the leaping stream, and held it there. "You may not get younger, Mama," he was said to have told her. "But by all the saints, I'll see to it that you never get any older."

The story is probably true. Whatever her fate, *La Vieja* had played her part, leading Ponce de León to the discovery of Florida. That done, she disappears from the pages of history.

Ponce de León's first visit to Florida occupied the spring and summer months of 1513. A great many false stories have been told about what he accomplished in that time. He did not found the city of St. Augustine. His only connection with it is that he made his first landing somewhere near where the city now stands. St. Augustine was built by another Spaniard, Pedro Menéndez, in 1565. That was fifty-two years after Captain Juan's land- ing, and forty-four years after his death.

Ponce de León did not find a Fountain of Youth at St. Augustine, or anywhere else. There is no sound reason for believing that he was even trying to find one. The story of his search for it belongs with the Washington cherry-tree legend. Like it, this is simply a romantic story which does not become true because many people have believed it.

# Back to Spain

THINGS had not gone well on Puerto Rico during Captain Juan's absence. As a matter of fact, they had not been going well since Díaz and Cerón took over the government. The two men were cruel, greedy, and ignorant. Under their rule, native Indians were being treated as harshly as those of Haiti.

Even the Ponce de León plantation had suffered. The overseers had fallen into their neighbors' ways. Work hours were lengthened, food rations cut. Doña Inez's gentle protests had gone unheeded. It was a sad story she had to relate to her returning husband.

Captain Juan went to work to set things right on his own estate. Even nature seemed against him. A hurricane swept the island, destroying crops and huts. It was followed by an outbreak of tropical fever.

On top of everything else, both Puerto Rico and Haiti suffered from raids by the Caribes of nearby islands. They came without warning in their swift canoes, looting the coastal villages, killing the men and carrying off women and children. The Spanish authorities, never knowing where they would strike next, were scattering their soldiers so thinly that effective resistance was impossible.

Cerón and Díaz were panic-stricken. They sent frantic messages to the King, urging him to give them more soldiers. When he did not respond, the governors asked Ponce de León to help them out. They knew that he was planning a trip to Spain. Would he speak to the King for them?

Captain Juan had no great desire to do favors

for these two men. But it was true that something must be done about the Carib raids. He promised to lay the problem before His Majesty.

His own affairs were the reason for the Spanish journey. He wanted to report his discovery of Florida in person, and make sure of his authority to return as governor. Once news of the new land got about, there would be plenty of Spaniards anxious to settle and rule it. The wording of the first grant had not been too clear. Ponce de León hoped for a new and stronger one.

He sailed in the summer of 1514. He would have taken his family with him, but Doña Inez was nursing the fever patients, and unselfishly refused to leave them. A small convent of Dominican nuns had recently been established in San Juan. With the aid of the good sisters, Doña Inez was doing what could be done for the stricken native families.

So Captain Juan returned alone to the land of his ancestors. He went straight to the home of his patron, Don Pedro Nuñez de Guzman.

Once there, it was as though he had never been away. Time and distance had not lessened the deep affection between the two men. Juan's welcome was that of a beloved son.

"I can give you little news, son Juan," Don Pedro said over dinner. "I wrote you of my new pupil, His Majesty's grandson Don Fernando. It seems strange that I, an active soldier once, should end my days as tutor to the royal children! But I grow old, and my fighting days are over. I lead a very quiet life. The boy comes to me for his lessons, so that I seldom go to court. The court itself is very different from what it once was. For me, nothing has been the same since Queen Isabella died."

"A sad loss," Juan commented. "It plunged even our distant islands into mourning."

"And saddest of all for our royal master. Misfortunes have fallen thickly upon him these past few years, Juan. His son-in-law, Don Philip, never ceases his insolent attempts to wrest the crown from him. And his daughter's madness wrings his heart. All this, and the loss of his dear lady—you will find the King greatly changed, Juan. Greatly changed." He sighed, and then added more brightly, "You have not met our new Queen. She will want to hear your tales of distant lands."

"I know nothing of Queen Germaine," Juan answered. "The French King's niece, is she not? We heard that King Ferdinand had married her for political reasons, to strengthen the tie with France. It is impossible that he should love her as he did the sainted Isabella."

"Impossible indeed. Queen Germaine has his respect and tender care, but Isabella had his heart. Ah, well! The new Queen is a charming lady, young, pretty, and very gay. But you will see for yourself when you go to court. Have you written for an audience?"

"Yes, and His Majesty has kindly set it for a day next week. I can only hope that he will approve my plans for Florida."

King Ferdinand received him at the appointed time. In spite of Don Pedro's warning, Juan was shocked at the change in His Majesty. When Juan last saw him, he was a hearty, ruddy-faced soldier in the prime of life. Now he looked old and worn, and strangely shrunken. Although he was as courteous as ever, his attention seemed to wander as Juan talked.

"Florida, Florida—a new land to conquer," he said fretfully. "And what is the good of all these conquests? They promise me gold, but where is it?

I have spent more gold on maintaining my governors and their armies than has ever come back to me. How do I know that there is gold in this Florida you speak of?"

"No one knows it, Your Majesty," Ponce de León admitted. "I do not promise it. If there is gold there, I will find it. But as for spending money —I am not asking you for a copper penny. I will explore and settle this island at my own expense. And with respect," he added carefully, "I would remind Your Majesty that when I was governor of Puerto Rico, it cost you very little. Given a few more years, I should have made the island self-supporting."

"Well, it's not self-supporting now," Ferdinand said angrily. "They're begging me for a new army out there. Tell me, what do they need it for? I can't make sense of all this talk about cannibals. I thought we had the Indians hard at work, and turning Christian. Are they turning cannibal now?"

Patiently Ponce de León explained. On the islands where the Spanish were firmly settled, the natives were working and giving no trouble. As to whether they were becoming Christian, he could only speak for his own plantation, where that was certainly the case. But the settled islands were ringed about with others, where the whites as yet had no foothold. It was the savage Caribes of those islands who were the enemy.

"Cannibals, are they?" the King asked.

Captain Juan shrugged. "So our Indians say. I can't vouch for the truth of that. But I know that they are fierce fighters, far more skilled in warfare than the natives of Haiti and Puerto Rico. It is true that they are raiding the settlements, and making life intolerable for our people."

"Thanks, Don Juan—this is the first time anyone has made it all clear to me. Well, what is your opinion? Must I send these fellows an army, as they ask? How big an army? Trained soldiers don't grow on trees, you know."

Captain Juan hesitated. "May I speak frankly, Your Majesty? It would take a huge army indeed to guard all the seacoast, as Cerón and Díaz plan. If I were in their place, I should not attempt it."

"No? And what would you do, then?"

"I'd visit the Carib islands, and try to make friends with them. Why should there be eternal warfare between the red men and the white? I'd do my best to make them see reason."

"And if they refused?"

"Then, of course, it would come to fighting. But I'd do the fighting there, on their own islands. Even if they were not completely conquered, I could give them such a lesson that they'd leave us alone. Let them stay and be cannibals if they must, so long as they keep away from the white settlements. That seems to me the sensible plan."

"But even for this, you'd want an army," the King said thoughtfully.

"Not a new army," Juan answered. "There are enough soldiers on Puerto Rico for such an expedition, if it went straight to Guadeloupe. That is the savages' principal stronghold. One sharp lesson there should stop the invasions, for a time at least. Of course," he added, "this is my idea, not that of the two governors. Their thought is to defend the coast. For that they would certainly need more men. But in one way or another, something must be done to stop these raids."

"Well, your plan seems to me the better one," the King said. "I'll think it over. And now, I suppose you want to get back to this Florida matter.

If, as you say, you are not asking for money, it is soon settled. Go back, by all means, and bring this new possession into Spanish control."

Juan waited a minute, and then said resolutely, "To do that, Your Majesty, I must have firm authority to rule it in your name. My present grant refers to the island of Bimini. I would respectfully request a new one, naming me royal governor of Florida."

The King smiled. "And why not? It shall be drawn up and signed at once. And now, Don Juan, I should like to take you to the Queen. Her Majesty will be amused to hear of your adventures."

Juan drew a long breath of relief. It had been so easy, after all! With a light heart, the new governor of Florida followed the King to the quarters of Queen Germaine.

The young Queen and her ladies found Captain Juan a most entertaining companion. They shrieked with laughter over his tale of Ortubia and the magic fountain which worked no magic. The more tenderhearted of them shed a tear for the poor old Indian woman and her hopeless search. And they playfully made him promise to ship them a bathtubful of magic water if ever he found it.

Captain Juan, his business done, would gladly have taken the next ship home. It would have been better if he had. But Don Pedro urged him to stay awhile, saying mournfully that this was probably their last meeting on earth. It turned out that he was right, for the good old knight died the following year. It was also Juan's last meeting with Ferdinand, who was only two years from his deathbed.

So Juan stayed on for several weeks, having a very pleasant visit. But some time in those weeks, King Ferdinand had an inspiration. He had been impressed by Juan's plan for a campaign against the Caribes. He had decided that Juan himself was just the man to lead it.

Ponce de León heard the news with dismay. He wanted to get on with the Florida scheme. He wanted nothing to do with Cerón and Díaz. He certainly did not want to go to war under their orders. As politely as he could, he explained this to the King.

His Majesty had a ready answer. The two adventurers had done a miserable job as governors. Diego Columbus could no longer take it as an affront if they were removed. Bluntly the King put it up to Juan. He would go to Guadeloupe and subdue the Caribes. When that was done, he should have his old job back. Governor of Puerto Rico and Florida both—did that appeal to him?

It could not help appealing to a man who loved power as Captain Juan loved it. He accepted gratefully. With only a trace of regret, he put away all thought of Florida and sailed home to embark on the Guadeloupe expedition.

Subduing the Caribes was not so easy as it had seemed when he outlined it to the King. The peaceful approach failed completely, as it had failed in Florida. It took two years of hard fighting, in which more Spaniards than Indians died, to win an uneasy victory.

Even then, the whites had to leave the Caribes in undisputed possession of their own island. All that was accomplished was an end to the raids on Haiti and Puerto Rico. These raids were resumed some years later, but not in Juan's time.

He came back from the fighting to his old post as Puerto Rico's governor. The job kept him busy for nearly five years. He loved this island which he had made his home. He was desperately anxious to see it peaceful and prosperous again.

Cerón and Díaz had left it in bad shape. Under

Juan's new rule, agriculture revived, the workers were looked after, new towns were laid out, merchants and artistans were encouraged. There were churches and convents to build, schools to be provided, roads to be graded and harbors improved.

Ponce de León did it all, and did it well. By unceasing and devoted labor he earned for himself the title of "Father of Puerto Rico." Over the centuries, right down to the end of the nineteenth, the people of Puerto Rico have had little reason to love their Spanish governors. They loved Juan Ponce de León, and they honor his memory even to this day.

# The Last Voyage

IT was the spring of 1521 before Captain Juan was free to return to Florida.

Months went into the preparations. Cattle and hogs were slaughtered, the meat salted and dried. Juan's experience with the Florida natives made him unwilling to depend upon trading with them for food. He tried to carry along everything his men would need until they had obtained a firm foothold.

This was not a voyage of exploration, as the first had been. This time, he meant to make a permanent settlement. His ships carried carpenter tools, nails, and farm implements. There were horses, cattle and pigs, and seed grains.

Most of the men with him expected to make Florida their homes. Once they had built the settlement, their families would join them. Captain Juan had given the preference to married men in selecting his settlers. All of them were, or had been, soldiers. They were well supplied with muskets, powder, and crossbows. Juan had no hope of taking peaceful possession. He had seen how fiercely the Florida Indians resisted the white men. He thought, however, that his expedition would be strong enough to deal with them.

As he had promised the King, Ponce de León paid for these lavish preparations from his own purse. The outlay came to a great deal more than he had counted upon.

After their disastrous Carib campaigns, Spanish soldiers were not too anxious to invade unknown savage lands. Captain Juan had to offer cash bonuses, as well as the promise of estates. In a letter to the King's successor, he wrote that he had "ex-

pended the best part of my fortune" on the enterprise. He was sure, however, that new wealth from
the new territory would make it all up to him.

The day of departure came. Ponce de León and
his men heard Mass in the San Juan church, and
then marched down to the harbor in a gay parade.
Trumpets and drums sounded, banners waved, and
crowds lined the street to cheer. Captain Juan himself, splendid in full armor, marched between two
missionary monks with their crosses. Christianity
and civilization were coming to Florida.

Doña Inez waited at the dock, in a crowd of
women and children. She had begged her husband
to let her go with him. "You took your wife and
child to Puerto Rico, and no harm came to us," she
urged. "I plead with you, my husband, do not leave
me behind."

Regretfully but firmly he had refused. The other
men were leaving their families. What would they
think if he made an exception of his own?

He did not tell her his real reason for barring
women and children at this time. The Florida Indians were very different from mild King Guaybana and his people. Ponce de León had had nothing but hostility from them. He expected noth-

ing less now. Until the natives had been pacified by force, there was no safety in the flowery land.

Tenderly now he took her into a last embrace. "It will not be long, my dear one," he promised. "Once we have the settlement under way, I shall return. Come now, dry those tears. I have left you so many times. Did I not always come back?"

She stifled a sob. So many times, indeed! To Higuey, to Puerto Rico, to the cannibal islands. Always she had waited at home. Always he had returned safely to her arms.

Why, then, did her heart tell her that this time there would be no returning? The tears came again as she clung desperately to him, whispering, "Do not go, my beloved—oh, do not go!"

He freed himself from her clinging hands.

"This is not worthy of you, my dear," he said reprovingly. "You are setting a bad example to the other women. You have always been such a brave little wife! Do not fail me now."

She dried her eyes and lifted her proud little chin. All around her, the other wives and children were wailing aloud. Doña Inez held up her hands for silence.

"My sisters," she said clearly and sweetly, "I am

ashamed of my tears. It is not for us to weep, but to pray. When the ships have sailed, I ask you all to follow me to the church. But for now—oh, we must send these brave men away in good heart! Smile, then, as soldiers' wives should. Let them see us smiling as they go."

The women responded quickly, hushing their sobs, twisting their tear-stained faces into smiles. The men hurried aboard. There was a cheerful fanfare of trumpets. The ships cast off, and moved slowly down the bay.

Doña Inez stood proud and straight, smiling and waving. Her tall daughter Isabel was at her side. With them were the two younger children. The boy Luis would one day follow in his father's footsteps as *Adelantado* of Puerto Rico. Captain Juan's descendants would spread throughout Spanish America, honorably bearing the name of Ponce de León down to our own time.

Captain Juan would never see his grandchildren. Watching until the little group faded from sight, he was looking his last on those he loved.

It had been decided to make the first settlement on Florida's west coast. This would bring it nearer to Cuba, and nearer to Mexico. Both Cuba and

Mexico, settled since Captain Juan's arrival in the Indies, were growing in importance to Spain. Mexico and later Peru would become the real seat of Spanish empire, providing the gold which the islands lacked.

A great deal of exploration had been done since Juan's first visit to Florida. It was now known that this was no island, but part of a continent. Mexico, another part of the same continent, had already yielded riches in gold and silver. There was every reason to hope that Florida would do the same.

No doubt Captain Juan hoped to find gold in Florida. But he had done very well on Puerto Rico as a planter. Gold was uncertain, but agriculture was sure. He would not be too disappointed if he could turn his new realm into a happy land of sugar cane and waving corn.

They sailed up the west coast to a point near what is now called Charlotte Harbor. Surveyed from the sea, it looked like the ideal spot. There was a bay, with water deep enough to take their ships.

Behind the beach lay the usual belt of trees. No Indian huts were visible, or any sign of inhabitants. Ponce de León gave the order to turn into the bay.

They did not go ashore at once. Captain Juan was moving with extreme caution, determined to guard against a surprise attack on the landing party. He waited a day and a night, keeping a close watch on the land. With his keen eyes he swept the tree-tops, watching for the smoke of cooking fires. None appeared. Except for the flight of birds, nothing moved in the empty landscape.

All signs seemed to show that this spot was truly uninhabited. So much the better. Once they got a stockade built, it would be much easier to repel an attack. Captain Juan did not doubt that the Indians would be upon them sooner or later. But he counted it a rare stroke of luck that he would have a little time to get ready for them.

He ordered the ships to begin unloading. Some of the supplies were carried ashore and stacked on the beach. The party built fires and cooked their evening meal. Sentries were posted, but nothing disturbed the good night's sleep which followed.

The unloading went on next day. Taking a strong party of armed men with him, Captain Juan went a little way into the woods. There he marked out the lines for a stockade. Men were set to work chopping down trees to build it.

It cannot be said that Captain Juan neglected any precautions. Although he honestly believed that there were no Indians near, he saw to it that his men kept their weapons with them. Guards were stationed around the clearing where work was going on. So far as the commander could assure it, the camp was fully on the alert.

These measures were good, but not good enough. They were no good at all when the attack came, at high noon of the second day.

There was no slightest warning. One minute the woods were empty. The next, they swarmed with painted warriors. They dropped from trees, they crawled through tall grass, they seemed to come from nowhere. The sentries had no time to cry out or to aim their muskets before they fell to spears hurled by unseen hands.

Captain Juan was on the beach, supervising the last of the unloading. He drew his sword and plunged into the fight, shouting the Spanish battle cry, "Santiago! God and St. James!" Dropping their burdens, the men caught up their weapons and followed him. Cannon boomed from the ships, stripping the leaves from the trees. The battle was on.

It was a battle which might have been won. Ponce de León had won more desperate ones in his time. The Spanish were superior in weapons, and probably in numbers. They were giving a good account of themselves when an Indian arrow caught Captain Juan in the thigh. He fell, and his men gave way to panic.

They picked up their wounded leader and carried him to his ship. Some unknown officer ordered the trumpets to sound the retreat. Summoned back by the call, the fighting men left the field and crowded aboard ship. The Indians danced threateningly on the sand, held back only by the menace of cannon fire.

Ponce de León recovered consciousness and demanded his sword. He struggled to his feet, shouting "Santiago!" in a feeble voice. Then he collapsed on the deck.

His terrified followers waited no longer. The ships put to sea with all haste. Since Cuba was the nearest land, they headed in that direction.

Captain Juan's wound had come from an arrow point dipped in poison. At first his followers had hopes that he would survive it. They could do little for him aboard ship, but they brought him safely to Havana, where skilled doctors were available. No skill could avail against the unknown poison. He died a few days after being brought ashore.

The governor of Cuba gave him a fine funeral, with full military honors. His body was placed aboard a flagship and carried back to San Juan, where a second funeral followed.

The islanders who owed him so much jammed the cathedral for the last rites. Doña Inez went through the long ceremony with white-faced composure. All her waiting was over, and all her tears were shed.

He lies now in the east wall of San Juan cathedral, in the city he founded and loved. Americans of the mainland know him only as the discoverer of Florida. But his own Puerto Rican people do not forget that he was truly the father of their beautiful isle. Approvingly they quote the epitaph his friends devised for him:

IN THIS NARROW GRAVE

RESTS ONE WHO WAS

LION BY NAME

AND

LION BY NATURE

# *Authorities Consulted*

## BOOKS

HARING, C. H. *The Spanish Empire in America*. New York, Oxford University Press, 1947

HATHAWAY, ESSE V. *Romance of the American Map*. New York, Whittlesey House, 1934

KIRKPATRICK, F. A. *The Spanish Conquistadores*. London, A. and C. Black, Ltd., 1934

LOWERY, WOODBURY. *The Spanish Settlements within the Present Limits of the United States*. New York, G. P. Putnam's Sons, 1901

MERRIMAN, ROGER BIGELOW. *The Rise of the Spanish Empire*. New York, The Macmillan Company, 1918

MORISON, SAMUEL ELIOT. *Christopher Columbus, Mariner*. Boston, Little, Brown and Company, 1955

OBER, FREDERICK A. *Juan Ponce de León*. New York, Harper and Brothers, 1908

PLUNKET, I. L. *Isabel of Castile*. New York, G. P. Putnam's Sons, 1915

# AUTHORITIES CONSULTED

## ENCYCLOPEDIAS

CATHOLIC ENCYCLOPEDIA. 17 vols. New York, Catholic
Encyclopedia Press, 1907-22

ENCYCLOPAEDIA BRITANNICA (14th edition). 24 vols.
Chicago, Encyclopaedia Britannica, Incorporated,
1954

# Index

# INDEX

# INDEX

Ponce de León, Juan: meeting with Don Pedro, 3-12; family background, 6-8; in Don Pedro's service, 12-16; sails with Columbus (second voyage), 30; returns to Spain, 40; back to Haiti, 41; courtship and marriage, 42-52; becomes governor of Higuey, 59; explores Puerto Rico, 69-77; governor of Puerto Rico, 92-5, 130; Bimini expedition, 106-16; discovers and names Florida, 109-111; last visit to Spain, 121-9; leads war against Caribes, 130; last Florida expedition, 133-42; death, 143

Ponce de León, Inez de la Torre (wife), 42-8, 55, 56, 60, 61, 67, 81, 84, 88, 90, 94, 95, 106, 107, 121, 122, 135-7, 143

Ponce de León, Isabel (daughter), 61, 91, 137

Ponce de León, Luis (son), 94, 95

Ponce de León, Rodrigo, Marquis of Cadiz (cousin), 7, 20, 21

Portuguese war, 16-18

Puerto Rico, 30, 31, 33, 63, 64, 66-8, 79, 86, 87, 93, 96, 112, 116, 117, 120, 121, 125, 127, 130, 131

Religion, 18, 24, 25, 55, 56, 60, 90, 135

San Juan, Puerto Rico, 94, 122, 143

San Salvador, 109

San Servos, Spain, 5, 6

Santiago, Father, 4, 5, 7, 9, 12

Santo Domingo, Haiti, 53, 59, 85

South America, 34

Spain, 16, 39, 121, 122

St. Augustine, Florida, 110, 118

Sugar Cane, 62, 93

Toro, battle of, 16

Valladolid, 16

A NOTE ON THE

## *Type*

IN WHICH THIS BOOK IS SET

THE TEXT *of this book was set on the Linotype in Janson, a recutting made direct from type cast from the original matrices cut by Anton Janson. Janson, who may have been of Dutch origin, purchased a foundry and was a practicing type-founder in Leipzig between 1660 and 1687. His first specimen sheet was issued in 1675. His successor, Johann Karl Edling, issued a later specimen sheet showing all of Janson's types in 1689. The Janson matrices were later brought to Holland, from whence they were sold in 1720 to the Erhardt foundry of Leipzig. Later acquired by the Drugulin foundry of Leipzig, they eventually passed into the hands of the Schriftgiesserei Stempel of Frankfurt am Main, where they are now preserved.*

*Janson is an excellent example of the sturdy and influential Dutch old style types that prevailed throughout Europe during the seventeenth and early eighteenth centuries. It is highly legible, and its individual letters have a pleasing variety of design.*

COMPOSED, printed, and bound by H. Wolff, New York. Paper manufactured by P. H. Glatfelter, Co., Spring Grove, Pa. Typography by Charles Farrell.